writing with cold feet

The Secrets of How to Write When You Are Not Writing

(for all writers, reluctant and otherwise)

Kathrin Lake

Praise for *From Survival to Thrival* also by Kathrin Lake

"Kathrin has created a great book for our crazy, chaotic world. She gives us compelling insights, as well as tips and techniques to live a more fulfilled life no matter what gets thrown at us."

- Michael Schell, Author of *Buyer-Approved Selling*

"Kathrin Lake is on a quest—to help you thrive! With vulnerability and insight she lets you in on pieces of her own journey, and shares principles and stories that have the potential to move you beyond mere survival. This book is filled with nuggets of inspiration and truth, followed up with concrete suggestions for action, many of which will alter your life for the better if you simply grab on and run with them."

- Darren Wride, Author of
Release: A Wilderness Adventure of the Soul

Other books by Kathrin Lake
The A to Zen of Writing
The A to Zen of Speech Writing
The A to Zen of Writing for Websites

Praise for Writing with Cold Feet

"When I am discouraged as a writer and about to give up Kathrin says exactly the right thing and I can turn to her anytime in *Writing with Cold Feet*. She also gives invaluable coaching in how to make characters come alive and challenges me to go deeper and develop the story line beyond what I initially wrote. I got my passion for writing back!"

- Ellen Chauvet, *When Darkness Falls*

"I wish I'd had *Writing with Cold Feet* in my 20s, when I stopped writing for reasons that seem ridiculous to me now. It's full of great how-to advice for beating self-defeat and kick-starting creativity. Especially love the passage about self-esteem - turns out, you don't have to have a tortured soul to be an excellent writer. Who knew?"

- Robin Spano, author of *Death Plays Poker*
and the Clare Vengel mystery series

"Kathrin addresses why so many of us approach writing with "cold feet" and tells writers how we can let go, and let our writing flow. Keep this little gem at your side as a trusted friend who's been there and can guide the way."

- Gordon Thomas, New York editor

"Kathrin has penned a thoughtful, honest and helpful companion that will be a true asset to your writer's journey."

- Stephanie Staples, author of *When Enlightening Strikes*
- Creating a Mindset for Uncommon Success

Buddha Press

For information on discounts for bulk purchases please contact
director@vancouverschoolofwriting.com

To find other books by this author please go to
www.kathrinlake.com
Book cover and interior design by Krista Gibbard,
Vancouver, B.C., Canada

Printed in United States and Canada

Library and Archives Canada Cataloguing in Publications
ISBN: 978-0-9881041-2-9

To all my teachers and students who gave me their best so that I could become a better teacher, a better writer, and a better person.

And, in memory of Mark Diamond, my teacher and mentor, whose generosity helped me believe in myself as a writer many years ago, and made a profound difference in my life.

Acknowledgements

No one writes or publishes books by themselves and I would like to thank a few people for their technical and moral support: Rosemary Wilson, Gordon Thomas, David J. Litvak, Jim De Haas, Karen Hadley, Krista Gibbard, and all the individuals who allowed me to use their stories for the greater good of teaching. Also, I would like to thank the people who have been supporting The Vancouver School of Writing in its inaugural year such as Elena McGregor-Rivera, Roger Killen, Peggy Richardson, Andrea Carvalho, Victor Mironenko, Nathalie De Los Santos, Gary Bizzo, Philip Ho, Julia Eden Vidakovic, Gail Z. Martin, Eileen Cook, Bob Mayer, and many others.

contents

3 Writing is Not What You Think (Secrets)

4 The Secrets of Letting Go

5 The Last Secret - Your Process

How *Writing With Cold Feet* Began

After graduating university and getting a degree in two Fine Arts disciplines, Film and Theatre, and with a few small playwriting awards under my belt, I started to teach creative writing to adults in night school. I researched and developed many original techniques to get the best from my writers, trounce their trepidation, engage their playfulness with words, share the art of making language simple but engaging, and help them understand the intricacies and secrets of story. It was the most rewarding part of my life.

After teaching for a number of years, the school came to me and asked if I could teach a class called *Fear of Writing*. Another teacher who had been giving the course was leaving and they had people signed up already. I said, "Fear of writing? I think I can handle that one," and took the assignment. But then I thought about it, what did I really know about fears? Sure I suffered from them, and lord knows I was familiar with my own anxieties about writing, but I didn't really know anything about what was behind them and what other writers were experiencing and what experts were saying. So I did some research about fears and anxiety and pulled together some terrific materials. I called my class, *Writing with Cold Feet*.

The great thing about teaching is that you are also learning, and it was from those first students that I learned that what we were experiencing could not rightly be described as a fear. We agreed that our "fear of writing" was a great deal more about procrastination. We just didn't always know why we were procrastinating. Off I went on more research to get to the bottom of this procrastination thing.

As a result of this research and more student feedback I eventually developed a new, successful course called *Putting Off Procrastination* and another course called *Putting Fear in Reverse Gear*. Both were for anyone suffering from procrastination, fears or anxieties that were holding them back. But working with writers exclusively was nearest and dearest to my heart, and as a Story Coach my focus has always returned to them. I have learned as much from the writers I have had the privilege to work with, as I ever taught to them. Some of their stories are included in *Writing with Cold Feet*, with their names and identities altered for anonymity. I hope their stories, and my own, and the ideas and techniques in this book will help all writers, and will-be writers, on their wonderful journey into themselves and the magical art of storytelling and writing.

introduction

Why We Don't Write When We Really Want To

Why? Why, oh why, do we procrastinate on our writing when we really want to write? What exactly is so scary about it anyway? This is an age-old question that I have been immersed in personally and professionally for many years now and I have finally consolidated my research, my answers and many stories. I personally hate to call it writer's block as it reinforces the ideas that writers have blocks, and even if we do, it is a very oversimplified idea, and also this phenomenon belongs to many kinds of artists and creative projects not just writing. That said, writers do have their special issues which this book is unique in addressing. I have put this not-writing phenomenon into five categories, there may be more to add, but for now I have found that they can be put under these five headings. While some may be what you expect, some are not. Many of these thoughts and knowledge about writing and writers are rarely talked about, dare I say they are secrets.

The first of the five headings that these secrets belong under is a double-barreled one that I call *Judgments and Feedback*. It may seem two pronged but really they go together indivisibly like law and order, rhythm and blues, Abbott and Costello. We fear judgment and judgment comes in the form of feedback. Seems simple enough but there are more angles to this than meets the eye or the ego. For instance, who is giving the feedback? Is the judgment valid? How do we know it's valid? If it is valid, should we listen to it? And who does this cycle of judgment and feedback effect? You may have mistakenly thought we would be discussing you, as the writer, receiving a judgment in the form of feedback, but equally, you can be the one dishing it out, and be on the other side of the coin for another. And, if so, what does that mean for your own feelings about judgment and feedback? Hmm. Yes, there are a great many creatures, even monsters, hiding under the rock that is judgment and feedback, whichever way it is presented. But don't be afraid, it will not be a deep analysis. What will be revealed will be useful and practical solutions, and wisdom for surviving and thriving in the face of either stinging or elevating feedback.

The next bucket of secrets is in the nature of our resistance to write itself under *Resistance and Other Pitfalls*. This starts with what is called resistance and rapidly moves to procrastination, but then moves into my top ten list of other pitfalls and reluctance to write (okay I didn't create ten, but trust me all the biggies are there). These are the perennial favorite excuses like "not enough time", "it won't make me any money" and "I have to do more research". For these, there are the secrets that prevent us from getting caught in our own webs of self deception, or how to get out of them when you see you are in one. It may be a relief to know that there are actions you can take immediately to interrupt your resistance.

There is one subject, a very important one, that really could have belonged in any or all of the groups, and that is your ability to see yourself as a writer. However, I felt it was best put it into the group I very deliberately called *Writing is Not What You Think (Secrets)*. To me, this is where the real secrets come out. People who have been writing for awhile may recognize some of these, though they may not have given them much thought. It is what no one ever told you writing was. Time and again, I watched my students and, at different points in my life, I watched myself, try to stuff our expectations of what writing and being a writer was into our efforts and come up short, frustrated and confused. It is ridding ourselves of these expectations and yielding to the true work of writing and being a writer that we can find freedom at last.

Or mostly. Then there are the lessons you have to keep learning and relearning --pretty much all of them—but none more important than the lesson of *Letting Go*. When it comes right down to it, all of it is about letting go. Letting go of expectations, letting go of judgments, letting go of resistance, but some letting go is more challenging than others partly because we are unaware of how tightly we are gripping to it.

Mostly, this gripping, is clinging to our own words. I realized that after a decade of teaching writing that I wasn't really teaching writing, I was teaching them how to share their writing. Sure I gave my students techniques that expanded their tool boxes in the craft of writing. I gave them structures, exercises, systems, and great tips too, but that's just information that gives them more choices, it is not what writing is to us as human beings. What they really needed was a place to start learning how to share their writing. Writing can be a lonely business, if you let it. To nurture the initial impulse to tell a story, to communicate a message, to impart something you see as important and to release it to the world is what most people are trying to figure out how to do, whether they know it or not. I know this is the age of the internet and blogs, so this may seem like a condition that is past its prime, but I am not talking about methods of delivery, I am talking about the psychic ability to let your work go out into the world and be what it may.

Finally, there will be the great summing up in *The Last Secret – Your Process*. This is about how to use all of this new, secret understanding to go forth and write with confidence. No, you will not be given a secret handshake, but you will be on your way to developing your own writing process. You will know it, and it will know you, and like any other relationship it will grow and change over time, and get easier and more familiar. By this time, you will have a lot of information on why you don't write when you really want to and a bank of ways to see the Truth, dodge the arrows, and keep writing.

Slow and Steady...

In my winter home in Mexico, the giant Tortoises, or Tortugas, lay their eggs in the sand each season and hundreds of babies are hatched. The people at the tortoise shelter will press into service any volunteer they can find to help release the babies successfully so that some will come back to the exact spot 15 years later and start an annual return to lay their eggs. It is a marvelous experience to be part of. When you are a volunteer you cannot help but be amazed at these babes, no more than an hour since they struggled from their shells, are so tiny that they fit into the palm of your hand. One day, they will be as big as a large coffee table, and some will live to 150 years old. But at the beginning, all a volunteer sees is a mass of hundreds of wriggling turtles in the bottom of a bin with sand. The tiny tortoises are trying to get to the ocean immediately, but many will not make it in the vastness of the Pacific.

The volunteers' goals are to ensure no birds will pick them off the beach, and to wade up to your knees and release the tortoises at the right time, right after a wave crashes, so that they will be naturally drawn out to sea and start their first swim with a very slight advantage. The first time I took part in this I could not help but be struck that only an hour after they are hatched these little things are ready for something as vast and dangerous as the Pacific ocean. Oh, if it were this way with human beings! And, what about writers? How often we are sent out with no preparation. So I use this book as my own way to launch you on your journey into the outside ocean of sharing your writing. I hope it will give you more than a slight advantage. One thing you can be sure of is that anything more you will need you will find in that ocean. Just keep swimming (keep writing) like the great tortoise swims and you will grow, live long and return to a happy shore to share you babies —your words— that will one day have legs of their own.

1

the secrets of judgment and feedback

Judgment

I often asked students to share stories of incidents that held them back from writing because many of us have these stories. They are the stories that underline a misunderstanding of writers and writing; they are stories of judgment and feedback, and how people deal with that judgmental feedback. One example of this kind of story is from Jill who came to my class in her early thirties. Jill had not done any creative writing since high school. Although she enjoyed it, she had completely stopped. The reason was one incident from school that was immediately, and very negatively, reinforced at home.

It happened that Jill had a sister who was just over a year older than her in age. They looked so much alike that they were frequently mistaken for twins and because of this they were frequently compared. Although this is hardly fair, it is a common occurrence in life to compare one person to their nearest contemporary, and as one of my favorite authors, William Goldman, says, "Where is it written that life is supposed to be fair?" To return to the story. Jill had handed-in a creative writing assignment in high school that she had truly enjoyed writing. When it was returned marked, it was not the grade she received that upset her; it was the written comment the teacher had made. It was just four words, "Good, but lacks sparkle."

Jill did not know what that meant, and was flummoxed, so she took it home to her mother in hopes that she could make something out of the comment. Likely she was looking for reassurance that this comment should not discourage her from continuing to write. Unfortunately, her mother did not help her fragile ego by saying, "Well your sister is the creative one, and you are the technical one."

Jill, being a typical awkward teen, struggling with her identity, accepted this. At least, for over ten years she did, but the call to write is not to be swept under the rug for a lifetime. And that is how she wound up in my class, hoping to write again and get beyond that feedback so many years ago.

It was stories like Jill's that made me always include in my writing courses a session on building up our fragile writing egos, and reenforcing our courage to write. Other than perhaps singing and speaking in public, people are in terror of being judged for their writing. They know they should want feedback, but they are scared stiff of it. Therefore, my session also became guerrilla training on how to accept and also give feedback.

Feedback and The Monster

Some of this training, to defend yourself against damaging feedback, I learned from my teachers in my acting training. My teachers in the Theatre, Penelope Stella and Marc Diamond, had labeled handling negative feedback as "How to Deal with the Monster." Who is the Monster? Unfortunately, the Monster can be anyone, and is often people who you both love and trust. They don't mean to monster you, but they do. It is often an offhand comment that stings and can hurt your creative self and throw you off. This is particularly critical to actors who have to perform the same scenes over and over again, and whose timing and delivery makes a complete difference to their performance, and to their fellow actors on stage with them. If they start to doubt their choices or their natural impulses as actors, the performance becomes contrived and soulless at best, and a nightmare of missed cues at worst, making their scene partners cringe. But writers are also vulnerable to shutting down and producing safe, soulless writing, or worse, no writing at all, because they have been monstered by someone's feedback, or simply fear it.

How do you protect yourself from the monster? First, know when you are vulnerable and it is coming. When you have put something out into the world, you know you are vulnerable, and sometimes you can see the feedback is coming from a mile away and other times it is an ambush. When you know that it is coming you can prepare, but when you don't, you still have to be prepared. And sometimes, we ask for the feedback, as Jill did from her Mum, and unwittingly sting ourselves. That is why it is good to learn quickly who the monsters might be. That is rule #1 about monsters. Identify them.

There are people who we can count on for good feedback that truly enlightens and inspires us. It's good to know them and consistently return to them. But there are also those whose comments are frequently well meaning but useless at best, and at worst, they keep us up at night building back our self esteem. We know these monsters from their history of feedback on just about anything. Your new haircut, the color you painted your apartment, the movie you liked and they didn't. Those who tend to give the critical comments up front, for almost anything, are the monsters.

When you see the monster coming, go into evasive action. Interrupt, avoid, find an excuse to leave, or some other action. If you have to engage, be direct, "Sorry, I am not taking feedback today, do you mind reserving your comments about my work." If the direct style is not your forté, or just not possible, you need to master how to receive feedback. All of us need this because not all feedback is expected, as in the ambush, but also, not all of it is evil. Some feedback is encouraging and positive, and if not positive, it may be constructive and useful, but sometimes you need to recognize which is which. All of us are going to easily let in the positive feedback, but there is that constructive feedback too, and often it comes wrapped up in the same package. If you care, you are probably going to want to discard the junk and store away the precious nuggets of constructive feedback and use them to build a better craft. But how do you recognize what to keep and what to throw away?

The first thing to ask when you receive some feedback is, is it general or specific? I asked Jill if "lacks sparkle" was clear and specific feedback to her. She said it was not and precisely why she had asked her mother to help explain. "Lacks sparkle" is a general, ambiguous, judgment and exactly the kind of critical feedback you should ALWAYS, WITH NO EXCEPTION, IGNORE.

Now, if Jill's well meaning high school teacher had said, something like, "Your story was good, but I was curious and wanted to know more about your main character." That is what we would call specific feedback, and feedback without judgment. The reader is simply telling you their valuable experience. You will also notice that good feedback takes longer to explain than a few words, such as "lacks sparkle." Valuable comments take a considered and analytical approach which repeats the merits of your writing and what you may be trying to communicate, and then looks at what may be missing, or needs reinforcing to make it more successful. Really valuable comments ask questions. Let me say that again, Really Valuable Comments Ask Questions. Questions like: "Why did you put this passage right after this one; was there a connection I missed?" "Why was the character so angry?" "What was the relationship of these two?" "What was the significance of this part?" "Where do you stand on the issue?" A question can reveal very clearly if something is confusing this particular reader and may confuse others. A question can tell you that you may want to add something, subtract something, or use a better device for communication, like an example or a metaphor.

You may want to ask, would this have to be another writer or someone with knowledge to give you useful feedback? Yes, I would answer, that may be a good choice for someone to give you feedback, except for one thing. Other writers can be just as notorious for being monsters. In that case, rule #1 of identifying who are monsters, still applies. But monsters may be unknown quantities, and even *you* may be a monster to someone else. So this section is just as much about you giving specific feedback, as it is about you receiving it. However, to get back to which feedback you should keep. After determining that the person giving it is not on your monster hit list, after noticing that the constructive feedback is specific and not general, the next step is to look at who, from a readership perspective, it is coming from.

Ask yourself if this person is who you are writing for? Is this your target audience? Is this the person who you want to reach or inspire? Is your writing to their taste? If not, perhaps you can ignore it and focus on the people who are gravitating towards what you have to say. In fact, always give yourself the option to seek out your audience and those who appreciate your words. If your writing is truly for everyone, then you should have an interest and perhaps a certain duty – although I use that word tentatively, as it is always up to you to make that call in each situation – to listen to what at least some of your audience thinks or feels. The layperson reader, or even an expert, may not be specific, and will often be both judgmental and general in both their praise and their condemnations. Therefore it is up to you to sift through those comments.

Thick Skin, Thin Skin

A local playwright and mentor of mine used to say, "In this business [the arts], you have to have a thick skin and a thin skin at the same time." In other words, you have to listen to your feedback with your armor on, and choose what you will take in. The general and specific rule is a good one to start, but given that your audience will often not know how to give specific feedback, you often have to listen and then it may be your turn to ask questions. Questions like: What was the most memorable or useful information to you? Was there anything I didn't cover that you were expecting? What specifically didn't work for you? Did this inspire you? How? Was there anywhere that dragged in the storyline for you? Were you clear about the… (insert point here)… that I was trying to make?

Coincidentally, several years after he told me his sage advice about a thick skin and thin skin, the very same playwright was hired by a Theatre company in which I was the General Manager. We loved his work and there was no problem with it, but at one point he decided to change the title of his play. The new title offended one of our major sponsors greatly. You may say that funders should not be controlling artistic license. Normally I would agree, but since these particular sponsors were marketing experts and had done focus group work with our intended audience (teens) for this project, it was not to be ignored.

I made arrangements for all of us to get in a room to discuss the title issue. I knew that the playwright was determined to exercise his artistic right to name his work, and the Artistic Director felt bound to back him up. I started the meeting summarizing each side's points of view, but also reminded the playwright of his own thick skin, thin skin advice regarding feedback that he had given to me years before, and letting him know how it had made a difference to me. He had forgotten he had told me this and was surprised that I had remembered. The reminder helped open him up. He listened. He asked questions. The fact that the sponsor was coming from a place of researched knowledge of our teen audience was the kind of feedback that he did need to have a thin skin about, let in, and digest. After our discussions, the playwright stuck to a title that everyone was happy with, and the play was a hit with our target audience as well. It was the win-win that everyone is looking for.

Don't Be the Monster

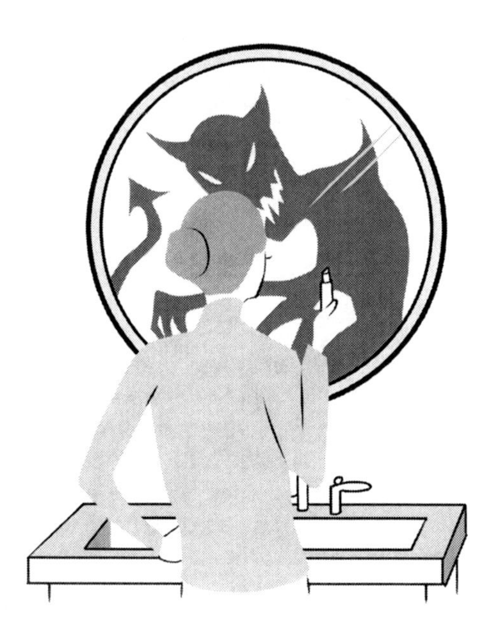

There was a writer I knew who I eventually avoided for numerous reasons, not the least of which was his criticism of others work. Now, he would never, ever, confront an artist to their face, it was always behind their back, or he targeted well known public figures, writers and artists, with rather vicious attacks of their work in which there was little room for appreciation. This is easy and safe for any and all of us to do. And we will. But should we keep a check on it? I think so, but not just because it's polite.

It didn't take long for me to wonder what this writer was saying about my work behind my back, but I also recognized he was likely his own worst demon as he tried to develop his own work. When you are highly critical of others you also tend to be highly critical of yourself at some level. Being critical of others to make yourself feel better about yourself is an immature and bitter path, but more than that, it forces you to be just as critical with yourself which can be a huge block. Wanting to do the best you can, and being self critical are not the same thing.

When I talk to prolific and well published authors, I find that with little exception they all love their own work, and they also appreciate others work. I see this as a mark of someone who has built a level of self esteem. Not to say they don't have their doubts ever, but by and large they are their own best fan. As one well published author told me, "I always thought that I was just wonderful; the cat's pyjamas!" Self esteem is a critical part of being able to take and give feedback and it also ties into thwarting your procrastination.

Self Esteem

Self esteem is a subject I have been keenly and personally interested in for a long time. In my book, *From Survival to Thrival*, I argue that it is an essential core necessity for living a thriving life. I also make the distinction that self esteem is often confused with self confidence and they are not the same thing. A writer, or anyone, may be confident and even cocky, but that does not mean they have high self esteem. Bravado does not replace nurturing self love, compassion, inner strength and kindness.

In my writing course, during the section on judgment and feedback, we often did an exercise that was a basic self esteem building exercise. After we did the exercise, I gave them a quick assignment to write on the spot for 15 minutes or so. At the end of that time, we would share our writing and I often saw something in each person's writing that I had not seen before. Something surfaced that they had withheld until then, and seemed to be released only after they had taken the time to nurture their self esteem. It may have been a greater vulnerability, or greater capacity to think outside themselves, or a passion that they now felt more confident to reveal. Indeed, after that class many of the students seemed to gain their momentum, and both writing and sharing became easier for them.

Many brilliant writers in history had horribly low self esteem, addictions and troubled minds. I am not saying that talent and low self esteem go together any more than high self esteem and talent go together. What I am saying is that the story of the tortured artist, is not predestined, it is a choice. And, if you have a choice, you are going to prefer to go through a writer's life with a healthy self esteem rather than floating on the highs and lows of confidence. Judgment and feedback are much easier to take when you are able to be compassionate to yourself, forgive yourself easily, and can be your own best fan through thick and thin. This is not a trait, it is a habit.

A healthy self esteem is like a healthy body, it relies on habits. We have exercise and balanced diets for our health, for self esteem it is self-talk. What are you telling yourself that you need to stop? What could you be telling yourself consistently instead? Can you say, I love my writing and I am the cat's pyjamas? Even if you don't feel your writing is fully developed yet, are you allowing yourself to embrace its own unique beauty, plain or elaborate as it may be? Love it, and yourself, wherever you are right now. Loving yourself is a process of self discovery and writing is a profound way to discover that self and honour it. I can't think of a better, and all around more useful way to deal with fears of judgment and feedback than working on your overall self esteem.

We also know that people who have lower self esteem issues procrastinate consistently, and that includes their creative work. I will touch on that again briefly when I get to procrastination. For now, it is enough to know that your reluctance to write may be helped simply by working on your self esteem generally.

There are many more secrets to learn about writing with cold feet. Your job, in this book, is to pick out the ones that will aid you the most.

2

the secrets of resistance and other pitfalls

Resistance

Resistance. What is it exactly? It is that initial malaise of "I don't want to do this," or "I can't do this, not today anyway." We just don't want to start. It is when the blank page, or even returning to the text we have left unfinished, seems daunting and dreadful. Let me make a distinction however, I do not consider resistance to be full blown procrastination, I only consider it to be the potential start to procrastination. Resistance is our own anxious unwillingness to get the ball rolling. The secret about this is that most people who are not professional writers think that only amateurs feel this. Not so. Everyone feels this at some time or another, or even daily; it is universal among human beings. Let me tell you a story that well-known Canadian choreographer, Judith Marcuse, told me when we were discussing resistance one day.

Marcuse had it in her head that she wanted the backdrops to her new dance pieces painted by a somewhat famous artist. The artist was, at this time, quite advanced in years, so she was unsure if he would take her commission. Judith is a very determined woman and contacted his wife and made an appointment to meet with the artist at his home and studio to convince him. On the morning of the meeting she was greeted at the door by the artist himself. As is polite, she said, "How do you do?" and was surprised when she did not get a standard response but instead he replied, "Not well at all." Judith, being a very caring and concerned person, asked what was wrong. He answered, "I have lost the will to paint." Judith's heart plummeted at hearing this pronunciation. Nevertheless, he invited her in, introduced his wife and then left the room for a few minutes.

While he was gone, Judith turned to his wife and said, "I don't want to distress you, but your husband just told me that he has lost the will to paint."
"Oh that," said the wife, "He says that every morning."

Woody Allen said that 80% of success is showing up. I used to think that he meant showing up to an appointment, a job interview, or an audition. And it does, but not only for those structured opportunities, showing up means taking the time to work through the initial resistance and get the ball rolling in your work as a writer. Whatever, your negative resistance mind tells you, whether it says that you have lost all will, or you just can't do it today, or that you don't feel well, or that you are afraid, or you have emails to get to, or whatever else you come up with, you listen and then you show up anyway. You just start. This may sound a little like the Nike slogan, *Just Do It*, but this is more about your own awareness that resistance is normal, that everyone goes through it, but it is just that, something to go through. But here is the secret about resistance. It only lasts three minutes.

The Three Minute Rule

To be honest, it may not last only three minutes, it may be less, it may be more, it varies for each person. However, what we do know is that it is usually a spectacularly short amount of time. And this is the secret solution. First, be aware when you are in resistance, and then make an agreement with yourself to start and work for three minutes only. I have a little dollar store timer expressly for this purpose: making time commitments with myself. In the case of resistance it usually takes only three minutes of starting for a person to become so engaged that they no longer want to leave. If you felt sick before, often you miraculously start to feel better. If you had been tempted to check your Facebook, clean your home or watch TV before, suddenly that seems far away and long ago. This is the three minute rule. However, you must have integrity, as with any agreement you make, if after three minutes you don't want to continue, you should stop as per the agreement, and do something else. So far, in my life, I have never stopped, not once, I have always kept going. The timer goes off; I shut it off and am totally engaged in what I am doing, and continue writing, often for hours.

As I said, it may be a different amount of time with you. You can experiment. It also means that whatever writing you start on, you don't have to start exactly where you left off, or exactly what you had intended, you are allowed to start on anything to get the ball rolling. Just show up, as Allen says, and make your way sideways to your goal. Or sometimes we start from someplace different and it completely transforms our initial intention and happily so. Sometimes you can genuinely see one project bite the dust and another emerge that holds the true fire for you. The point is, it doesn't matter what you start on. And if it is an essay, article, chapter or report you have to hand in on a deadline for school or work, hopefully it is relevant to your topic. But maybe today what will come out is the story that is worth failing a class for, or quitting a job for. Strange things can happen when you give yourself three minutes and break through the resistance to see what is on the other side. We will talk more about this when we discuss your Muse. You thought that was a myth didn't you?

So that is resistance, and the three minute rule is the only way I know how to solve it. But, what about that full blown procrastination that I was talking about? Time to tackle that one now.

Procrastination

Full blown procrastination is part of a vicious cycle that comes from the anxiety that we all feel in the post-industrialized modern world. Procrastination and anxiety are linked. We procrastinate because we feel anxiety, and then we feel bad about ourselves that we procrastinate on things, so we feel more anxiety. In this way, procrastination and self esteem are also linked. But where does this vicious cycle start? How can we, as human beings and as writers, interrupt it?

Procrastination starts from anxiety and the anxiety comes from our big brains. Bigger than any other mammals, our human brains have the ability to remember far into the past and project into the future. No other animal has demonstrated this amazing capacity. It is the secret to our success as a species and also the clue to our anxiety.

Because of our brain capacity, we remember every failure, not for moments or days, but years. We can project what may happen in the future and are just as inclined to project negatively, or troubleshoot, as we are to project or visualize positive outcomes. Many of us focus on past failures or project what could go wrong, and this freezes us. Sometimes the thought of success and what it might open up is scary. This is what produces the anxiety and tends to be enhanced from living in a world where we are given too much information, too many images and have overwhelming possibilities.

We see images of success that may be tempting, but are also horrifying, and the worst of celebrity nightmares. We are taught that even creativity is rated and has failure (which is a lie), and therefore people live in fear of experimenting or sharing because they may be making a "mistake." "Mistakes" are deviations from the norm and unfortunately are not thought of as groundbreaking new perspectives, or, at the very least, the learning opportunities that they really are. Instead, mistakes are seen as strikes against a person. In short, this is not a world where creativity is always embraced, so it is no surprise we have anxiety around this and therefore procrastinate.

Addressing true procrastination is where the *Just Do It* Nike slogan is actually harmful. Or as one researcher into task avoidance - as they call it in some academic circles - said, "To tell a chronic procrastinator to just do it is like telling a chronically depressed person to just cheer up."[i] Fortunately, most of us don't describe ourselves as chronic procrastinators, and even if you do, you can continue to apply your three minute rule, allowing yourself to stop at three minutes, as it will help. But do not push yourself, or beat yourself up. Use the feather, not the whip. More anxiety, the experts tell us, just makes the situation worse.

But doing nothing is not the answer either. If you recognize that you are a person who feels or generates worries and anxieties around many things, you may want to work with a professional. There are also excellent books. One book I recommend is Dr. Linda Sapadin's, *It's About Time.* From these books you may get a clue of what your pattern of procrastination is and how to best deal with it. Frequently it asks you to look at your self esteem and how you treat yourself under multiple situations. Low self esteem is a common thread for true procrastinators. For writers, I have found that there are a handful of possibilities that you may be going through that are deeper than initial resistance. I want to now describe typical procrastination scenarios that you may recognize and take the first step by being more aware.

If you find you are a chronic worrier and worry a great deal about what others think about your writing, then you may need some coaching to assist you. You may need someone who balances the "what could go wrong" with the praise and encouragement you need to go forward. Nothing replaces the loving support from a partner or good friend. It is priceless, but you still have to share with them. That means you are going to want to find positive people who believe in you, and avoid the monsters. There are also support groups from writing courses, writing groups — the pros and cons of which I will discuss later — and then there is working with a coach and a writing coach if possible. You do need to learn how to share your writing, and much of what you read in this book should help you let go of some of that worry. Many people came to me thinking they wanted me to correct their writing so they didn't have to worry about it, when in fact they only needed their first experiences in sharing their work in a monster-less environment to show them that they really had something worth communicating, or in the case of one closet poet, that the way they could communicate was truly recognized as beautiful.

Perfectionists can get stalled on starting and also on finishing because they get caught up in the details that are not so important, but they fool themselves into believing that they are important. That is how they procrastinate. Perfectionists who want to write may need to look for a mentor who gives them the permission to experiment, to take risks, to make mistakes, to put the details aside, to start (or finish) without knowing everything, and even to be bad (more about that later). Again, the info in this book, especially in letting go of your expectations of what writing is, and what writers do, will be helpful. Because, dear perfectionists, while grammar is a wonderful thing, writing is not about grammar. While having the newest technology may be nice, again this is not what writing is about.

Perfectionists also tend to have a fear of wrecking it, which we will also address as a common pitfall under the Pitfalls section. But essentially, perfectionists need to be willing to indulge their creative right brain and tell their detail-oriented left brain that they can get nit-picky later, much later. It is a habit they need to develop each time it comes up. Often creative games can help the perfectionists I've worked with, to distract them from the crippling disability of details and fully engage their playful, sloppy right brain. James Elroy who wrote *L.A. Confidential* seems to have an uncanny knack in his process to indulge his left brain by writing 120 page outlines and then, switch to his right brain to create eloquent, playful prose. Then, switch again to be the editor for rewrites. Not many of us can do this so easily, but it is a question of habits and there will be more ideas to consider in future pages.

Some people have an inherent need for a deadline and they thrive under pressure and the adrenalin of it. The whip cracking is what they are looking for. If this describes you, then you may be a person who would like to enter writing contests and enrol in courses with deadlines, but to be truly free and be the master of your own destiny, to be a self motivated writer, you may need to learn how to love the joys of doing a little bit at a time, and to push yourself rather than relying on external pressures. Adrenalin does not mean you are doing more, or investing in a quality performance in your writing. Time to rewrite is important. Appreciating the joys of writing without the adrenalin push may be your greatest lesson.

I know a couple of journalists who have been talking about writing a book for years. Being professional writers you would think this would be easy for them, but they are also deadline junkies and to commit to a longer piece of work over a longer time with no 11th hour deadline hanging over them is difficult for them. The subject is also suddenly personal and the objective style they are trained in isn't going to be appropriate. Without the adrenalin, pressure, or even the support of others in the news room, they are stuck. The book is on endless delay. If this describes you, there will be other information in the upcoming pages that may ring true for you and assist you in your challenges to battle this kind of procrastination.

The person who procrastinates by doing everything but their writing I will call the "yes" person. This is the writer who says yes to everything and everyone but themselves and their own creative heart. "Yes" people tend to have either a focus problem, a prioritization problem, or a people pleasing problem, or a little of all three. If this describes you, you need support too, but support from people who support your right to say no. And then, you need to learn how to assert your own boundaries around your creative time. You need to allow yourself to be absolutely manic about not being interrupted during this time. I had a DO NOT DISTURB sign I would put on my bedroom door when I had roommates. If any roommate disregarded that sign and walked into my room while I was writing, usually to ask a mundane question like, "where is the mustard, I can't find it?" — it was never anything critical — I refused to answer them. I would continue to focus on my computer, my book, my page, or the ceiling, until they got the idea and left.

Another possibility to some people's writing procrastination is that they have a dream that writing is going to be much easier than it is. They think that writing is like talking and it should just flow out perfectly with no effort or editing involved. As Truman Capote said, and he was a very good talker, "That's not writing, that's typing." Or, all good writing is rewriting. It does take effort, focus, and yes, some knowledge. You should look at what makes good writing succeed. Therefore, it is work. Some people have a hard time reconciling that.

I have one friend who keeps thinking (fondly) that he can hire a ghost writer, and he can. I have already given him advice on how to hire writers, however, the ghost writer still has to be told what this book is about, what the central story or stories are, what is the wisdom to be included, and how it should be portrayed. You may enjoy a collaboration, many do, because, as I noted before, writing can be a lonely exercise. However, you still have to mine the information and find the relevant stories yourself. It takes effort. You can use almost as much time working with someone else as it takes to put the words on the page yourself. And, to work with someone else, unless it's an unpaid partnership like your friend or spouse, will be much more expensive. And if it is your friend, sibling or spouse, you always run the risk of damaging that relationship due to artistic differences.

Everyone who cares, has editors and proofreaders at minimum, but that comes later, the writing is still your work. So if you are procrastinating, hoping that the effort of writing will somehow change, it won't. The good news is, it is okay to ask for help, and the better news is, there can be a lot of joy in the effort of writing. But it is an effort.

So that is my take on writer's procrastination in a nut shell, but there are more pitfalls for reluctant writers yet to come. I will try to include more stories at this point so you can see how these resistances play out and how they can be overcome. I will start with the two biggest lies we like to tell ourselves in regard to writing, and those are about money and time.

Money and Writing

Money and time are the two most dominant, pervasive challenges, excuses, or blocks to writing that I know of. If one or both of this deadly duo has not surfaced for you yet, you are not living on the same planet as the rest of us, or possibly you are independently wealthy, with no duties or responsibilities to anyone, and have an enormous amount of free time on your hands. That's our fantasy, right? Guess what? Those people are not writing either. So time and money are excuses. And, because this duo is just as powerful as singular forces as they are together, they deserve individual attention. Let me start by telling a true story that may help you as it still does me.

Decades ago, when I was in university, I had a roommate who invited me to her parents place for dinner one night. I knew that her father was a writer. Some sort of journalist I thought, because I knew that he travelled to Europe frequently. Her parents lived in an amazing house, high up on Burnaby Mountain with a beautiful view of the inlet they call Indian Arm. The house was large, and of classic West Coast design that was meant to blend into the surrounding forest. To make more of that point, they had even built their back deck around a large evergreen tree which, in effect, poked through a hole in the middle, fully preserved as a natural feature of the house's harmonious design. The inside was tastefully decorated; bright, modern and had numerous inspiring photographs of nature on the walls.

I found her parents charming, warm and curious about our studies. Her father and I seemed to hit it off. During our conversations at dinner my roommate made a point of telling her father that I was doing weekly poetry readings at the university's open mike night (long before they had poetry slams). I saw her father's eyes light up and he asked me more about my poetry and my interest in poetry. I said that I loved performing poems as the spoken word because I felt that was the best way to express the rhythm and soul of the poem. He agreed and seemed enthusiastic about my thoughts and peppered me with more questions. Finally, he asked me what I intended to do with my poetry, beyond university open mikes. I said I had no plans for the poetry, and added, "It's not like I can make any money from it." "Kathrin," he said with a twinkle in his eye, while he gestured around the room to the whole house, "poetry paid for all of this."

Although I am no fan of clichés, my mouth did, in fact, drop open. As it turned out, my roommates' father was a well known poet in Europe who had published numerous books and had frequent speaking engagements where he read his poetry. His books were often large, coffee table books because they were accompanied by full color pages of his own beautiful color photographs of nature. They were, of course, some of the very same photographs that adorned the walls of his house that I had noticed when I came in. He also produced beautiful wall calendars that were immensely popular, combining photos and poems. Although most of his books were initially written in German, his mother tongue, they had been translated to many languages, including English, and before I left that night he gave me a copy of one as a gift which I still have in my library. His name, if you care to investigate, is Ulrich Schaffer.

I often think back to that evening and think that even though he was living proof that the starving artist, writer or poet was only a reality if you bought into it, it took me many years to really disconnect myself from that myth. I still perpetually remind myself that you can do what you love and make a living at it, if you are willing to work towards it. You can indulge your creative heart. You don't have to buy into the mythologies. Indulging your creativity isn't without its challenges, but life is filled with challenges anyway.

I have discovered that all artists are entrepreneurs and the sooner you recognize that, the sooner you may surrender to acquiring some business skills, like marketing. You are wise if you keep in mind these three things: learn any skills that can help you, surround yourself with supportive, wise and admirable people, but above all, if you are going to get there, you need to be persistent and stick to it, or always return to it. Keep sticking to these three things and you will find a way. Even if you are having parallel careers for years, or you do most of your writing after you retire from your non-artistic career, you can still make it the joy and center of your life. But, if you dwell on the idea that it will never make you enough money, you are simply diving headlong into a pitfall that most of us hide in for too long and then emerge from wishing we had more time.

The author, Tom Robbins, says that he was never so happy as when he and his first wife, having committed to his writing career, had to steal vegetables from someone's garden in order to eat. Giggling and snickering in the night like a couple of kids, it tided them over for a patch until the next thing came along and Tom's writing and books really took off. If you are in a place of uncertainty, not able to see the future, then the adage, the mantra, the affirmation I recommend is "faith over fear." Choose it every morning and recognize that it is okay to begin to prepare a different path that is less consistent and takes time to build.

If you can take comfort in others' money struggles on the way to their path, then read about them. In fact, there are about as many ways to take care of the money angle as there are authors. Everyone does it differently. But the ones that never become authors are the ones who told themselves repeatedly I can't do that because, as I said to Schaffer, I can't "make any money from it." Don't buy in, keep writing and keep figuring it out.

Time and Writing

Just as there are as many ways to deal with the money angle for writers, every writer deals with the time angle differently. One famous, best-selling author used to get the kids to bed, and go to bed for a few hours until 1 a.m. She woke up to write from 1 a.m. to 4 a.m., then back to sleep, got up at 7a.m. to get the husband and kids off, and then went off herself to work part time in an office, came home, had a nap, and then got ready for everyone to come home and do it all over again. That is how she says she got her three hours of writing in every day. She also acknowledged that she hired a maid, but even with that support, most of us could not do this, for many reasons. But some of you may.

Personally, I find that I can get only piece work done while I face a day job or day-to-day life. In order to finish, or make great progress on a larger work, I have to go away and focus on it. Brendon Burchard calls this chunking. I call it retreating.

I love the word, "retreat," not as much for its military fallback reference, although there is a certain freedom in realizing when you are beaten and daily life is kicking the hell out of your creative life, and you have to get out. The real reason that I like the word "retreat" is more child-like. It is because it has the word "treat" in it, and "re" in front of it means you are treating yourself again! I really treasure my retreats; they truly are treats. I don't struggle. I don't have to force myself to do my writing, I simply enjoy it. Yes, I go through resistance, but essentially I know how precious this time is and how it changes me, for the better.

When I say it changes me for the better, I mean that when I allow myself a creative life, I look at things differently. In retreat, I am not tapping away at the computer constantly or pondering text at every moment, but when I exercise my creativity consistently and daily, my heart starts to break open. I first noticed this when I squirreled myself away to finish a play. I got up, ate breakfast and looked at my printouts from the day before and made corrections and edits on the hard copies (I don't do edits on hard copies until the very end now), then I would make the edits on the computer. After that, I would start on the new text, jumping from the computer to lying on my bed and staring up at the ceiling and letting my characters whisper to me, and then back on the computer. Then I would take a long break, eat, and go for a long walk. On this walk, I started to notice that I had changed. I felt entirely different physically, emotionally and psychically. I looked at things differently. After indulging in my right brain, I sometimes felt almost moved to tears at the beauty I saw. And I saw beauty in everything. The colour someone had painted their front door. The leaves in the trees and how the breeze moved them, and the sound the two made together, was a symphony to me. I felt connected to everything around me and was moved by it.

When I got back from these quasi spiritual walks, I went back to work and worked for another couple of hours. Ate my dinner, maybe wrote a little more, and then I would write in my journal about how my writing day went before I went to bed. I would wake up and do this all over again. This was my process and it has changed somewhat over the years but this experience of joy and connection still exists as a happy side effect of using my creative brain. I think my story is important because we must remind ourselves how joyful it is to exist in your creativity. If you go to that place that says this project is a task to complete like any of your other daily tasks, you will at best resist this process, or at worst you may destroy this special creative world and its possibility. Stephen King, in his autobiography about writing, said that his alcoholism wasn't sad because it prevented him from writing books, it didn't, it was sad because he couldn't remember writing some of them. He knew how much he enjoyed the process of writing and he feels like he missed that magical time.

Was every moment of my writing process so peaceful and harmonious? God no! My first subjects, like so many young artists, were essentially two things, pain and loss. And I had to go to these two crummy places frequently. I once complained to a woman who was a guru teacher in the Theatre, a woman who is one of the few people I know who can both talk a mile a minute, and who can also listen deeply and profoundly and who actually hears what people are really saying. Rare to find in one person, her name is Linda Putnam. I said to Linda that all my work was about pain and loss and I was becoming afraid that my whole life might be spent dealing with pain and loss in my writing. She said something infinitely simple but equally true, she said, "Make a choice."

Wherever you find the time to write, remember that you are treating yourself to this creative work, and it is work, but it is also a treat, and it is also your choice. So enjoy it and discover what it can be. Will this enable you to create more time? No. In physics, creating more time is a complex theoretical idea and considered an impossibility to do, especially while staying on this planet. Will you make a choice to *find* more time? Possibly. Finding more time is always a possibility in human physics. It means giving up something else. Whether it is something frivolous like watching T.V., or something precious, like spending time with friends and family, something has to change, and a sacrifice may be necessary. Do you have the courage to go into your boss's office and ask for a 3 or 4-day work week, and take the cut in pay if she or he agrees? That is all it really takes to find time, to acknowledge that a sacrifice is called for, and then to take action.

By the way, at one time I did ask my boss for a 4-day work week in order to write and he said no. However, not long afterward a recession hit, and, along with many others, I was put on a 4-day work week. It seems that if you have the courage to take action, and make the commitment to finding time, the universe is impressed and often helps you along. As Carl Fritz, a writer and artist I met in Mexico told me, "You can always make more money, but you can't make more time." Part of what you may want to learn if you don't know already, is how to enjoy your writing process. Don't dread it, and by committing time to it, understand that things will start to fall into place.

Research

OMG, I love research! It's like being a detective, you get to dig up more and more fascinating information. For those of you who are bookworms (and not all writers, or will-be writers, will describe themselves as book worms), you probably love to plough through dozens of books and gather information like a squirrel with nuts before winter. The problem only comes when we keep researching and we don't do any writing.

Whether you are writing fiction or non-fiction, research can be a seductive phase that writers don't want to let go of, or sometimes never feel they can do enough of. Here is the secret: you don't have to do all your research before starting to write. You don't even have to do half of it. Some even say you don't have to do any!

Oh yes, myself and 200 other writers did an intensive four hour course with two successful science fiction writers who described research as a big whirlpool that they see many a writer get sucked into, never to return. This, they said, is not good for the writer. A writer has to write and free themselves from anything that may stop writing as a continuous process. Now, I started to be convinced that they were on to something, until they suggested that no editing should be allowed as well. They may have a point for first drafts , however, I have learned that their writing style and my writing style lived in two different worlds, with two different readerships. Their process was not my process. But, I had to agree after watching myself, my students and other peers, that getting lost in the research angle was possibly one of those things that looked like you were working, but really you were procrastinating from the scary part: to put words on a page.

I have heard professionals suggest a method for writing speeches and papers by suffusing yourself with so much research and so much knowledge that it will flow out of you easily. This is possible. I am not suggesting that there are not benefits to this method, however, having been in Toastmasters for about 15 years now, I can tell you that I have seen too much research ruin as many speeches as too little. Even for fiction research, which may be based on real facts, or it could be constructing fictional back-stories, can start to take on a life of its own. When all is said and done, for any written work, whether it is meant to be heard or read, a person may use only about 10% of their research. Often it informs the confidence in their writing more than the content or the quality.

So how do we know when to stop researching and start writing? Well, here's a thought, why do you need to finish one in order to start the other? Why can't research be done as a back and forth process? In other words, you do your initial intense research, start writing part of your piece, then do more research, maybe in the same day, and go back to writing, and then back to research to pick up what you need, and then go back to writing again. Sure you still may have whole sessions just dedicated to research, but if it is balanced with whole sessions where you are only writing, you can be sure you are not using research to procrastinate on the writing. At some point the research should narrow to random fact checking, and all your time should be spent at the word processor.

The internet is both handy to use for this back and forth writing/research method, and it can also be that great whirlpool that my science fiction writers warned against. It is easy to see fascinating links when perusing the internet for information; this is less of a danger with books. While sometimes these side trips can be serendipitous, more often they can waste a great deal of time. Most experienced authors of fiction and non-fiction have learned what the correct balance of research and writing is for them. Most of them describe their first books as having far more research than their later books. This does not mean one book was less researched than another; they just became much more able to pinpoint their research and waste less time and effort on it. This is knowledge that only experience can provide but for now you need to ask yourself, am I a research addict? If so, it is up to you to wean yourself off the research and spend some time constructing sentences. You can always go back.

Chronology

One of the secret pitfalls of new writers is that they think they have to write chronologically. I love the story of J.R.R. Tolkien, the author of *The Lord of the Rings*. He was an academic professor and had no idea how to write fiction and did not have any fiction writers around him when he started on his epic trilogy. Consequently, he began at the beginning and started writing. Each time he got stuck he would scrap all of what he had written and start from the beginning again. He started the trilogy three times and almost wrote two full books that were completely scrapped using this method. Most writers would never have continued on, but as one expert said, because Tolkien had come from the unknown horrors of WW I the first modern war, in a culture where men did not speak of such things afterward, he had acquired a "narrative debt" so deep it sustained him through writing and rewriting his book in this chronological fashion.

If Tolkien had been connected to a community of fiction writers and been given a bit of training on the process of writing for fiction, he may have realized that you don't have to write chronologically. Many, many writers of fiction and non-fiction, myself included, don't ever begin at the beginning. I didn't with this book and I don't expect to for my next book. Where do we begin? Usually whatever part gives us the strongest pull or images in our mind. The part that gets you excited and you want to share the most. After writing that part, we may write what comes just before, just after, or somewhere in the middle.

When I was a student writing essays, in order to get me started on a paper I would write what I would call a bogus beginning. It was an opening that I knew I would never use and would change completely later. Why did I do this? Perhaps it helped break my resistance, but more likely I was still tied to the idea of the chronological process. It is perhaps logical to think that if you read it chronologically, it had to be written that way. Slowly, you learn that this is a limiting way of thinking, and not how the creative right brain chooses to do its best work.

Sometimes our resistance is compounded by the left brain voice that says, "But, I don't know where to begin." What our left brain that orders things means when it says this is, the beginning of our piece isn't clear yet. But it doesn't need to be. Listen to the right brain instead. If you sit with it for a moment, sit with your thoughts quietly, there will always be one part, one idea, one example, one phrase, one scene, often an image or it can even be one word that is clear. You start there. I remember a powerful moment when I was working with a writer and I witnessed him have a breakthrough as we were talking. Suddenly, he found a piece of paper and wrote in big letters across it: TRUST. This is where he began.

Wrecking it

Have you ever written a beautiful line, or the beginning of a story, or the start of an essay or article that you were kind of excited about, and even proud of, damn it. Then shortly after you finished your great beginning and were admiring how clever you were, you froze. Your cold feet crept up to your head and gave you a chilling thought, *what if I wreck it?* And the voice continued: *It's too good right now, if I keep going there is no way I can maintain that level of writing. I can't match those clever turns of phrase all the way through. I am not sure where the next thought is coming from. I am not sure where the plot is going. I'd better just put it away until I am inspired again. I really, really don't want to wreck it.* So there it sits, a promising start, in a drawer, never to see the light of day.

Sometimes our Muse gives us some really juicy material and it flows out so easily that we can barely believe it. Then that flow either disappears or, more likely, is frightened away by our fear voice. Here's what you can tell the "I don't want to wreck it" fear voice. Remind them that you can't wreck what has already been written. However, going forward, accept that it may not all come out so easily or "perfectly" but that is okay. Why? Because the Muse is impressed by work and if you keep going, often, if not always, your muse will eventually come back to you. There will be more info on the Muse later, but for this particular pitfall you have to remind yourself that getting to the work part is the part where others shut down. Only the writers who will eventually publish (either self-publish or by traditional means), keep going.
It is your choice. You can either be content with being the only reader of your wonderful beginning, or keep going, and dope out the next steps, finish it, and share your words with others.

There is another technique you can try for this pitfall, and it is reverse psychology for writing. Try to wreck it. Start writing to wreck. Experiment. Start a new page that continues on your last thought and try to let it be shallow or stupid. Don't be surprised if you actually find this difficult. Also don't be surprised if it gives you some really great insights to whatever you were writing about. In short, you can use the 'wrecking it' voice against itself. The contrarian attitude opens up your mind from conventions and often moves it to wit, humour, poetry and some more advanced operations that you didn't know that your brain was capable of. I have a cartoon on my computer in which the character says, "Saying intelligent things is not really difficult, just think of really stupid things to say, and then say the opposite." Make the 'wrecking it' voice your ally and not your enemy, and it usually goes away on its own to leave you to move forward confidently where others fear to tread.

Finishing

So many people come to me with unfinished work that they have stalled on. Sometimes they have stalled for ten years. Is all hope lost? No, but I don't recommend allowing that stalling to happen for that long if you can help it. In this section, what I want to address is why it may have happened initially, if you should start again, and how you can get it underway ASAP. I will also discuss the phenomenon of those who do not even start because they are afraid they won't finish (because this has happened to them before).

There is nothing more painful than to label yourself as the person who doesn't finish things. Oh the lashes we inflict on ourselves! We tell ourselves horrible lies: we are lazy, we are unfocused, we cannot face our fear, we don't have time, we will never make it work, we've lost the will, lost the inspiration, we will wreck it, and whatever else our insecurities can dredge up. Here's the secret on this one. Well, two secrets. The first secret is that sometimes you are not meant to finish it, so stop beating yourself up. A creative mind has a plethora of ideas that are almost like entities unto themselves, but some survive and some don't. Nature is like this, it produces many so that one will survive. Like our baby tortoises, many eggs, many hatchings, only a few live to a ripe old age. It is like this when you are brainstorming in a group. The group may come up with many ideas but only settle on a few.

I watched a fascinating show where they asked authors this very question, have you ever abandoned a book half written? Many of them had, and for some it had been a huge weight off their shoulders to leave it behind, and for others it was still a painful memory of loss. However, all of them moved forward to the next project, the one that was meant to be. So, be prepared to let some projects go and know with utter confidence that nature will provide you with umpteen more ideas, projects and starts that may or may not stick. The most important take away from this first secret (that not all starts are meant for finishes), is that beating yourself up is a useless, damaging exercise.

That was the first secret, the second one is only a judgment call from the first one. What if you decide this story, this piece, this book, this one is meant to survive? What if you have put a ton of sweat equity in already and it has still stalled? The secret here is that you are in a relationship. You are in a relationship with your writing like it is your lover and the relationship has cooled for whatever reason. You can go to counselling. Which means get help from a teacher, writing coach, or mentor. Or, you can find the fire that started you in the first place. Or you can even try some time apart, as distance sometimes makes the heart grow fonder.

If you are stalled on a long term project, be it a book, a memoir or a thesis, then ask yourself a few questions. What was the spark at the beginning? What do you want to communicate so desperately? Why was it so important to you personally? Has that changed? Maybe you got bogged down in a part that was too heavy? Maybe you thought you had to write it chronologically? It is actually less important to know why you stalled and more important to get back to the original idea, thought or scene that gave you that initial spark. Reconnect with that energy. In effect, rekindle the romance.

Similar to Julia Cameron's idea in her book *The Artist's Way*, you can take that energy out on what she calls an Artist's Date. Take it out to see creative works of art, and feed it the creativity of others. Writers tend to be readers and will read those authors that inspire us and give us permission. But if we are intimidated by others' writing as well as inspired by it, perhaps you can read another genre than the one you are writing in. See if there are other kinds of creativity that you can be inspired by. For example, for some reason I get inspired by contemporary dance which is abstract or interpretive. I don't understand it, I don't even have to really enjoy it, but often I find myself digging a pen out of my purse and trying to surreptitiously write notes on the back of my program in the dark. My Muse does like it. Ask yourself how this artist or this piece of work might inform your work. I don't care if you are writing a business book, it is still a creative process to tell a story, and communicate your passion effectively.

I know authors that find photos, create a collage, or put a talisman in front of them that visually reminds them of that spark. This can help enormously. Writing is a temporal art; it happens over time and not like a visual art piece that we can grasp in one view of the eye. This is why when in the midst of writing, it can feel like a forest you are lost in. One Pulitzer prize-winning writer, Jon Franklin, calls the getting lost part spaghetti-ing. It happens to the best of us. If you are lost, then follow the smoke back to your fire. If it still confuses you what to do next, then the answer is to pull out all the threads you are weaving and find the main one that this is really all about.

I remember being lost while working on a play back in my "pain and loss" writing days. I wrote down in big letters on pieces of paper all of the themes that were emerging. One word or theme was written on each piece of paper that I taped the ceiling of my living room. I lay on the floor and stared up at them trying to will myself to make sense of it all. This was not a bad technique, but if I had known then what I know now about the brain, I would have tried to add images with my words. In any case, after staring up in frustration for some time I decide to just start writing randomly whatever I wanted, whatever came to me. I had just started down a promising path when I looked from my office into my living room. The tape on one end of the pieces of paper had failed, and the paper was now hanging down vertically like a pendant flag. The word that hung down like a real sign from God was DEATH. As chilling as that may seem, it happened that this was the theme behind the promising path I had just started, and in a stroke of insight I could see clearly it was the main thread of the entire play. Death, and its multiple purposes and possibilities, whether it was pain and loss or transformation to make room for the new, was the theme that jolted me back to life. Once the main theme was clear, my words flowed. Once again, the universe seemed to be working mysteriously in tandem with my efforts.

The point of this story, is to do something, do anything, do something wacky to break your block. Don't do this by doing the exact same thing. Take some time to go back to the fire to stoke it again. Maybe you already know your main theme, or maybe you will have to look at all the strands you have branched off on since you have been spaghetti-ing. Be prepared to sacrifice any and all of the strands to get back to that main thread again, which should also be your fire. Then, combine this process by putting new words to it. Let the reignited fire drive you as it did when you first started. The romance is rekindled.

If you are a fiction writer, this process will also involve reconnecting with your main characters in a deeper way than you have done before. Remember this is about relationship, and those with your characters are important ones, but this will be dealt with more in the next chapter *Writing is Not What You Think Secrets, under Characters and the Evil Puppet Master.* For now, we only have one more brief pitfall to address in this chapter, Others.

Others

We have already discussed Monsters under *Feedback and Judgement* but there are always Others. Others can be good and they can be bad. You may want to write for an Other. You may want to stop writing for an Other. You may find you want to write, but Others get in your way. You may have an Other who inspires you and is your Muse personified.

If you have given Others any power over you and your writing, you may want to examine if that power is positive or negative. You may want to examine if that power is real, or you have fabricated and nurtured it. If it is positive, and this person inspires you, this may work out just fine. But are you dependent on them? Would you feel unable to write without this Other? If it is negative, you may want to ask yourself if this Other should even have a prominent place in your life?

However involuntarily it may be that we give some people power over our writing, whether it is to impress them, or to prove to them, or keep them happy, or put our writing dreams on hold for them, it is good to be conscious of where you stand and with whom. The ones who you feel no threat from, and no danger from being monstered by, you should definitely keep around. The ones who you fear, whether it be their judgment or something else, you may want to figure out how you are going to handle them, and start on the process of liberating your power from them and putting it back in your hands, and your pen. For now, just be conscious. You may want to make a list of people closest to you, or even at a distance, and choose if they are your writing's enemies or allies or a neutral Switzerland.

The great importance of Others is that we have to acknowledge, sooner or later, that we do our writing for them. And we need them. We need their reaction, their praise, their smiles, their sighs, their laughs, their tears, their ahs, their confusion, and their feedback on what they got out of our words. We build on this. We build our ego, our craft, our thick skin and our thin skin, and we do it all over again, for them.

The Universal Antidote of Lists

If after all this, you are still feeling resistance, your procrastination has got you, and you are in a pitfall that you can't identify or overcome, try the universal antidote. Start making a list. A relevant list. A positive centered list. For example you can list all your themes. List all your stories. List your characters. List your characters traits and habits. List your points. List ideas. List your thoughts off the top of your head. List who your writing allies (not enemies) are. List your writing accomplishments. Just start with a bucket of lists.

You don't have to do anything with them but throw them into the back of your head and mull them over. The idea behind lists is to start with something easy and non-threatening. No one is afraid that a list will be judged (or I hope not). After that, just wait for the first impulse to come, and it will, today, tomorrow or the next day, one of those words on the list will return and you will pick up the pen (for three minutes) and write. Or perhaps you will just start to organize the lists until you get that impulse. Have faith and make a list.

What Makes You Love to Write?

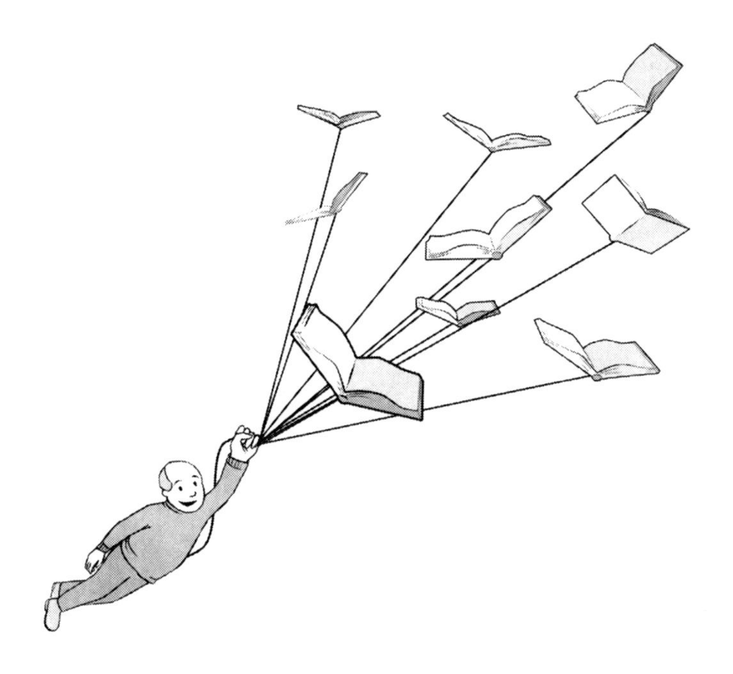

So far this chapter and this book has been all about what makes you stop writing, your resistance and procrastination, but it would be very damaging if I didn't remind you of something very important: you love to write! I assert that you would not be reading this book if, at some level, you did not love to write. Even if you are shaking your head right now saying "no, no, no I don't like it," consider that the voice inside your head telling you to shake your head who insists on disliking writing is the one who struggles with writing, but there is another person in there who loves it. How do I know this? Because I have had the sentence "I don't like to write" said to me many times before, and have seen it completely transform to, "I really enjoy writing," and even, "I love writing!"

How does this happen? I like to think that I touch on so many aspects of writing during a coaching session, writing course or retreat that everyone finds a chance to fall in love with their writing again. We don't all love the same things about writing, but finding out what you do love and what compels you forward, is a great gift. Once you find out the things you love about writing, then you can better make sure you are including them in your writer's journey.

I have always been highly suspicious of Dorothy Parker's quote, "I hate writing; I love having written." I think the highly quotable Parker was doing just that, coming up with a good quote. I also recognize that in her quote is the seed of what compelled her and a lot of us to write, and that is that for many of us the sharing of the writing is the best part. I would be very surprised if there were not many other aspects of the process of writing that Parker enjoyed, but the biggie for her was likely sharing it. It is not unheard of for people to change their minds about the things they used to dislike about writing once they start doing them enough, however, to begin with, you have to include what you do love and make sure you get a good hit of it in your life.

I have included a list of some things that people say makes them write, and what they love about writing so that you can check off the ones you recognize in yourself, and even rank them in importance for you. Are you getting enough of it in your life? If not, you have to figure out how to get that with your writing, and I will discuss a few points of how to do that after the list.

What Makes You Write

(and what do you love about it)

- ☐ Telling a good story
- ☐ Curiosity… on a journey to answer some question.
- ☐ Going into different worlds
- ☐ Learning how much wisdom I have
- ☐ Sharing it with others
- ☐ Transforming myself
- ☐ Getting to play someone else (or several others)
- ☐ Creating characters
- ☐ Discovering what I can come up with
- ☐ Escapism
- ☐ Wordplay

- ☐ The challenge
- ☐ Honouring history
- ☐ Getting to use fun verbs
- ☐ Creating metaphors
- ☐ Telling the truth (Truth)
- ☐ Communicating clearly and effectively
- ☐ Seeing more than what's on the surface (poetry)
- ☐ Making people laugh
- ☐ Being passionate about ______________________________
- ☐ Wanting to share a message
- ☐ Wanting to share wisdom
- ☐ Wanting to share a vision
- ☐ Wanting to help or inspire others
- ☐ To explore what ifs…
- ☐ Sharing what I've found out
- ☐ Honouring life
- ☐ Trying to make my peace with humanity and life
- ☐ Having an audience in front of me
- ☐ Entertaining others
- ☐ Recognition and (positive) feedback
- ☐ Having readers who love my work
- ☐ Personal satisfaction
- ☐ Hoping I can write a bestseller or make money
- ☐ My own healing
- ☐ For my family and friends
- ☐ To correct a great wrong (redemption)
- ☐ To impress ______________________________
- ☐ To give me purpose
- ☐ To be known
- ☐ To get revenge
- ☐ Other: ______________________________
- ☐ Other: ______________________________

You may notice on the previous list that some things are about the process of writing, and some are about the motivation to write, and some are about the results hoped for when sharing the finished product. It is not essential to have desires in all three of these areas, but I think it does help to have something that can be enjoyed while in the process of writing such as wordplay, using fun verbs, creating characters, the challenge, telling a story, or even communicating clearly. But, if your biggest thrill, like Dorothy Parker's, is to either share the writing, have positive recognition, or to entertain others, then you may need to do what I had to do: get in front of an audience sooner.

For me, this meant live performance. I know, this is the #1 fear, but for others it is also the #1 high. I have done theatre, poetry readings, stand-up comedy, story tellings and public speaking, despite shaking knees, sweaty palms and quavering voice (and sometimes I still have these) because the high of getting immediate feedback was too necessary to me. Therefore, I have built into my life places to perform as well as places to write. What can I say, I am a social animal.

How might you get what you need in your writing? With the internet, it is often easier than it's ever been to get yourself out there and start a readership, if that's what you are after. If you want to make money and have a bestseller, you have another kind of study in front of you, and marketing will be part of it. It also means it is pretty hard to sustain your enthusiasm while you are trying to accomplish your goal because it can take a long time and may never come. This is a huge failing for many. Again, look at what you enjoy about the process, or if you crave recognition or to entertain, perhaps you would like blogging and to share your writing as you work on it, and still stay away from public speaking. On the other hand, you may discover that writing is great, but making videos is your true high. You don't have to do a live performance for a video, but you can still get some feedback on the internet.

If you prefer to be totally anonymous, you may be satisfied with doing your writing for personal satisfaction or healing. Personally, I find that most people, despite what they say, have a deep inner need to share their writing or share themselves, even if the idea scares them silly. If you look carefully at the list above of what makes you write, and it may be different for each project, you can better determine what medium you can use and how you want to share with others and who you want to share it with. The three important points are 1) to figure out what truly motivates you to write, 2) what parts about the process of writing you love, and 3) how you want to share your writing, especially if it is a big motivator for you.

So ends this chapter on the positive note of what motivates us to write, after we have reviewed all the secrets about resistance, judgment, feedback, monsters and other pitfalls. You may be starting to see how this writing thing is kind of multi-faceted. And that is a good thing. Because, you will never be bored and you will always have something to learn. The biggest secret, which you may be starting to glean, is that writing is not what you think it is, it never was. It isn't quite the same thing that you had thrust upon you in Mrs. Richardson's English class, or maybe it is a little bit, but you have done some expanding since then. There is more to this mysterious creative process called writing, and even more about the myths we have about that lofty title, "writer." And this is the uncharted territory we will next enter.

3

writing is not what you think (secrets)

Permission to Be a Writer

One day, I was invited to the house of a writing student for tea. She wanted to discuss a block she was having. This woman had worked her whole adult life in the court system as a court stenographer and was now ready to write crime stories from what she had been listening to, and inspired by, in real life. She showed me her writer's garret where she was doing her writing. She lead me through her outlines, her plot lines and what she had written so far, but ultimately she admitted, "I'm stuck." She desperately wanted to research the answers to a couple of critical questions that could not be answered in a book. One was about interrogations at the police department, and the other was about autopsies. She told me that she knew many policemen and also people in the coroner's office who would be able to help her, but she could not bring herself to call them.

"Why not?" I asked.
"Because," she said, "I can't suddenly tell them that I'm a writer when my entire, professional career they have known me as one of their colleagues. They might ask me what I've written."

I have seen this many times before. Those who are writing, but have not yet published, judge themselves so harshly that it holds them back. As I was figuring out how I might best inspire her, I looked around at where we were sitting in the garden.

I said to her, "Your garden is absolutely beautiful."
"Thank you, my husband and I are able to spend more time on it now that we are retired."

Then an idea suddenly dawned on me.

"Listen," I said, "when you go down to the nursery and you go to ask one of the gardening experts there a question, do they tell you that they are not going to help you unless you prove that you are a gardener?"

She laughed and sheepishly said, "No."

I went further. "Being a writer is like being a gardener. You are a writer because you do it regularly, just like a gardener is a gardener because they have been gardening, not for any other reason."

She said, "You're right! I have been writing every day, even more than I have been gardening."

Two days later she told me she had contacted the policemen she knew and found out about interrogations. And, she was particularly proud that through her connections she had a personal invite from the coroner to see a real autopsy performed. Perhaps this is not something most of us would be overjoyed about, but she was. She had broken through. She had given herself permission to be a writer.

Similarly, years ago I needed permission from one of my mentors from afar to be a teacher of writing. One day, I was listening to a tape from Natalie Goldberg, who wrote her now famous seminal book for writers called *Writing Down the Bones*. On the tape I heard her say, "Do not wait until you are published to teach writing." I had to stop and rewind the tape to make sure I had heard that right. So inspired, I marched down to my local high school/night school office armed with a writing resume I had fashioned, a letter from a teacher, and proof of a small playwriting award I had just won, I told them I was there to teach creative writing. To my amazement they bought it.

This was the beginning of the most enjoyable and rewarding career I would ever have, other than writing itself, and often more so. While I love to write, I love to interact with others too, and by teaching I am forced to better learn my craft. But would I have started if I had not received permission? As a teacher, I hope that one of my gifts is to give students that permission in hopes that they will give it to themselves. This Permission Secret is: You Are a Writer If You Write (or a teacher if you teach, or a gardener if you garden).

Ultimately, I want you to become your own writer, conscious of your own writing process and the techniques, systems and methods that work for you and you alone. As a writer, you are the ultimate maverick and however you write is your own mish-mash of ideas that you have learned, begged, borrowed or have created yourself. The whole package is your process, forever evolving, and uniquely yours.

Finding Your Voice

With your unique process is your unique voice. The first time I surveyed my students to see what more they may want to learn about writing, their answer surprised me. They said they wanted to know how to create their own writer's voice. In discussing this with them it was clear to me that they had decided that this was very important. Many were concerned that they didn't have one yet. I was surprised at this anxiety because I was sure, up until then, that I had experienced every anxiety and insecurity connected to writing that there possibly was. How could I explain voice to them? Let alone how to direct them to find one?

After some research, and pondering, the most true and complete answer came from a movie. It is one of my favorite movies. *'Round Midnight* is from the great French director Bertrand Tavernier, about a Jazz legend in the 1950s and 60s who was played by a contemporary, and since passed, jazz legend saxophonist, Dexter Gordon. Tavernier chose a great jazz legend to play a story about another great jazz legend because, in the case of Dexter Gordon, he had all the life experience right there. The movie is both a fictionalized tale and almost a documentary about Gordon and other African American musicians and artists of that period who went to Paris to escape racism. But in a broader sense the film is also about artists who are always working on their own art form and expanding it.

In the film, Gordon tells a story which is likely true. He says that after a gig, some guy comes up to him and introduces himself as a fellow musician and saxophone player. Then he starts to brag. He tells Gordon that "I play you, better than you do." Gordon smiles sagely at this incident, knowing the difference between style (voice) and technique. He then tells us, in his slow, husky, bebop rhythm voice:

"Style isn't something you pick off a tree one day... it grows inside you...until it is ready to bloom."

And so it is with a writer's voice. You cannot teach it. You cannot learn it. You may, and you will, beg, borrow, steal or genuinely create a few things of your own, but it will all contribute to what will become your voice and you will not need to force it, or worry about it. Just follow where your likes, dislikes, and passions take you, and then just accept what comes out of it. And that's what I tell my students. Keep writing, explore, have faith and voice takes care of itself.

The Muse

"I go to the studio everyday because one day I may go and the Angel will be there. What if I don't go and the Angel comes?"
- Philip Guston, artist

I have already mentioned the Muse and want to explain that further. The formal history of the Muse or Muses goes back to ancient Greece when there was believed to be nine of them. Nine lovely spirits that inspired artists and scholars in the important arts of the time: epic poetry, love poetry, lyric poetry, sacred poetry, history, tragedy, comedy, dance/song and astronomy. You may have noticed a lot of poetry in there; it was kind of the T.V. of the times. In any case, what is important is that these divine spirits were the ones that were believed to have whispered great ideas, prose or visions into the ears of artists, writers, scholars or scientists which these mortals then brought to life. Is The Muse a quaint, old notion with no place in our high tech world of science? If that is your first impulse, it may be something that you may want to reconsider.

As high tech as we may have become, ideas and creativity still come from the same place. The thing that is not so clear is where that is exactly. Does it come from the human mind, the human heart, or from some ethereal place? Are artists merely the mediums, the conduits for their creations? The conventional paradigm for the current day is that it comes from the human mind. Brilliant thoughts and ideas come from brilliant minds and those people are known as geniuses. Likewise, brilliant, creative works come from artists who are also often known as geniuses. But that's not how the ancients saw it, and there may be a very good case for returning to their way of thinking and embracing the Muse once more.

Elizabeth Gilbert, author of *Eat Pray Love* released a terrific sermon at a TED conference in 2009 arguing this very idea. Gilbert noted that the creative force was too great a burden to place on single individuals. In the past, artists who were struggling and not producing more than mediocre work could blame their Muse, their Genie (genius) which was a force outside themselves. If divine inspiration was not forthcoming, then it was because the Gods or the Muses were not visiting you and there was little you could do about it, except try to tempt them to holiday with you. Perhaps, Gilbert suggests, if you were not producing great works, then it could be thought that your own personal Muse was not particularly talented themselves, or at least was having a bad stretch. In any case, the artist was somewhat absolved from blame. All that was required of the artist was to show up (remember Woody Allen), and to try.

The Hawaiians have a similar belief in Huna. The people who practiced this Huna were the Kahuna, as in the colloquial phrase, "the big Kahuna." Huna was originally called Ho'omana. Ho'o means "to make" and mana means "life force energy." This creative energy is thought to be impressed by human effort. The teachers of this practice say that if you try something, if you make an effort, Huna will help you, much like what a Muse might do.

The quote that precedes this section suggests that Philip Guston, who was an expressionist artist born in 1913, believed that he had an Angel that was the source of his divine inspiration. Now it had only been a couple of centuries before him that this idea in Western civilization of the Muse, or Genie, very gradually started to be left behind. Rational thought became a dominant belief, and with it the idea that genius was due to the brilliance of an individual alone. But it wasn't an easy transition for people to wrap their heads around, no more so than for us to now embrace the idea of a Muse, Genie, Angel or Huna coming to help us. To illustrate what a confusing concept rational thought was in the late 1700s, enthusiastic petitioners for rational thought created a statue to the Goddess of Rationality and paraded it through the streets of Paris. To us, this may seem an oxymoron but to them the two ideas had to coexist. At least, for a time.

So, before things changed, artists, poets, and writers did not have to be brilliant all by themselves. They just had to show up. Gilbert suggests that at the time in history when we started to shift our thinking and believe that artists had to be responsible for their own brilliance, the phenomenon of the tortured artist also showed up. Artists became eccentric, addicted, mentally ill, temperamental, tortured, suicidal individuals whose histories we are very familiar with, and have now become the stereotype. Gilbert ponders if our paradigm shift inadvertently destroyed many an artist who could not take the divine creative burden on their shoulders alone. Instead, the "celebration" of genius individuals created celebrities. The burden of celebrity still destroys many an artist, the stories of which we see in the tabloid news daily. As a contemporary example, the flash of musical brilliance, Amy Winehouse, whose death at 27 years old in 2011 seems to have mirrored this very stereotype of celebrity. Would she still be with us if we were applauding her Muse instead of trying to get a piece of the artist herself?

To gain sanity for artists again, Gilbert suggests we go back to the Muse. She talks about how she and other artists are in the habit of conversing with their Muse at times, even negotiating, as a way to assist the process. I also find this very helpful to think of creativity as outside my control at times, and all I have to do is channel it and be there. This is particularly interesting when we get into character development and where I discovered, once again, that writing was not what I thought, and it's likely not what you thought either.

Characters and the Evil Puppet Master

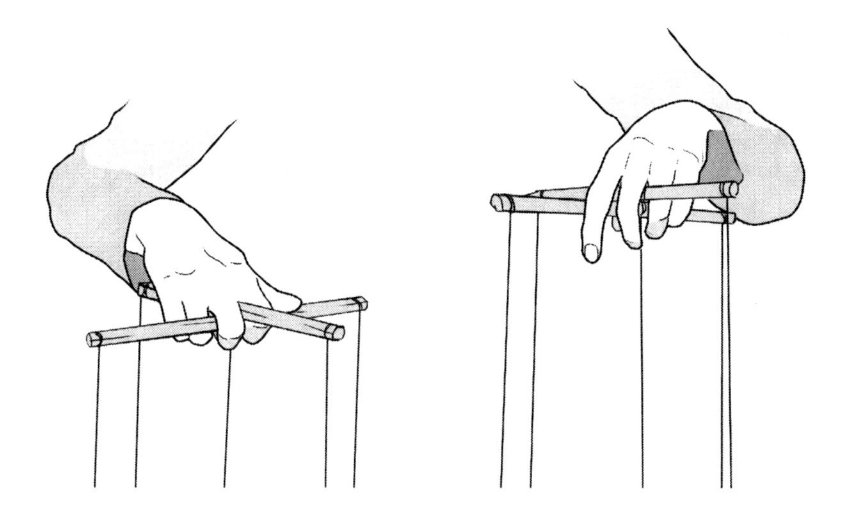

Probably the number one misperception of writing is that we want to think we are always in control of our own writing. If you want hum drum writing you can write in a very controlled fashion, but for exceptional writing you need to let go of control. Who do you give control to? One good choice is to your characters.

If you are writing a fiction story then you must never underestimate the power of your characters. If you are writing non-fiction, then characters should still be there, they are just interpretations of real people and often they include you. Your first question should be, why do you want to give control over to characters? Followed quickly by, how do you do this? You want to do this because characters (and your Muse) always lead you in the right direction. How you give your characters control is more complicated, but essentially it involves listening to them.

This will apply to fiction writers more than non-fiction, but there are lessons to be learned for both, and I will tie this in for the non-fiction writers eventually, so if that is you, bear with me. But first, let me tell you a story about an evening I was invited to many years ago for playwrights and screenwriters to test out their scenes using actors to play the parts. I wish I could attribute the author of this piece but it was many years ago and I long since lost the program. I am going to humbly try to recreate and paraphrase the scene here to give you a sense of what we saw, and if anyone can tell me whose work this is, I will happily attribute it.

Two men, friends, meet at a café, they are sitting together and one of them suddenly says,
"Oh, you know Frank? The character in the novel I'm writing?"
His buddy nods.

"Well, I just found out Frank is fat."
His friend looks puzzled and reflects on this for a moment before saying,

"I thought Frank was the character that was based on me?"
His buddy says, "He is."
His friend again reflects on this for a moment and asks, "Do you think I'm fat?"

"No! No, it's not you, it's just Frank, he's fat."

His friend again thinks about this with a furrowed brow for a few seconds and says,
"Well, can't you just make him thin?"
The writer responds.

"I've tried. I put him on diets, I made him do exercise, nothing works, he's just fat."

At this point in the scene, the audience, made up largely of writers, are laughing hysterically. Why are they laughing? Because this is a great illustration of one of the secrets of writing, especially of fiction, you are not ever in control completely, but your characters have a lot more control than you would believe. Your characters will want to do things that you don't want them to do, and have characteristics you don't like. And, try as you might you can't seem to visualize them any other way. Imagine how annoyed I was when, in one of my first plays, a central character turned out to be a chain smoker! I had long since been a petitioner against the evils of cigarette addiction so this was hard to take, but try as I might she really was a big time chimney. But this tendency for characters to have a will of their own is a very good thing. It means you are onto the best material there is, and the easiest writing there is.

When writing fiction, if I start to get a clear visual picture of my characters and hear the sound and quality of their voice in my mind, I know that all I have to do is to listen and let them play in my head. It's quite alright to have conversations with them too. Why not interview them? Whatever you don't know about them or their story, they will often tell you if you ask. And as far as the story goes, they are rarely, if ever, in error. I know this sounds weird and crazy and some people will have a greater comfort level with this than others, but this is the secret writers don't share with everyone (because then everyone might think they are crazy). Our imaginations, our right brains, are mysterious and when we get them working for us, they are very much in touch with a certain indefinable brilliance. It's not whether *you* are brilliant or have a brilliant mind but whether you can get out of your own way to listen to that brilliance?

It is a truth that many of the great characters in literature talked to their authors and told them the story. In 1921, the famous Italian Playwright, Luigi Pirandello, wrote a play that toys with this idea of characters being in control called *Six Characters in Search of an Author.* More recently, in 2002, the movie *Adaptation* by the screenwriter, Charlie Kaufman, takes a peek inside the writers mind and can be seen as the right brain and left brain arguing it out and personified as twin brothers played by Nicholas Cage. Is he going crazy or is it just the writer's process?

Control is another part of the illusion of what you thought writing was and how writers work. But, don't worry, you are still the ultimate master (sort of). It is up to you to figure out how to piece it together, like a mystery. So, if a character says that they are going to jump into that pool naked, it is up to you to later figure out why that is significant to their psychological make up, what it has to do with their story, and the story you want to tell. When you do, it is exhilarating. It is like being a detective and the clues start coming together and falling neatly into place. You may not always have to consult your characters, but when you are spaghetti-ing in fiction writing, if you ask your characters, they will often help you find the way.

Not all of it is as easy as taking dictation from your characters. You do have a lot of input, but what would be worse is if you did not listen to your characters at all. If you do not try to connect to them as they appear in your imagination, or if they do not come to you, you may be tempted to force it. It is then that you risk falling prey to what I call the Evil Puppet Master.

If you want genuine and believable characters or stories that people fall in love with, you cannot force them. The Evil Puppet Master is the control monger inside of you that wants to say: my character will now say this, act like this and everyone else will love them. Often, as writers, we cannot see beyond our own intentions or ego ideals. We cannot see when the work itself needs to lead, not us. But, if you listen, it can tell you what to feed it. This is as true for non-fiction as much as fiction. When our work, be it fiction or non-fiction, gets wrapped up in our ego, when we want to be loved, look cool or be authoritative, then we can be sure we are invoking the Evil Puppet Master.

As humans who create, we tend to project what our own ego ideally wants. We want to show no vulnerabilities and be as perfect as we can be in our fantasies. This is our ideal version of ourselves, but when we project it on to our characters it produces dry material and flat characters. Why? Because we, as human beings, are filled with frailties, vulnerabilities and flaws that everyone recognizes and needs to see. We need to see how individuals triumph over the world and their own shortcomings. If I had invoked the Evil Puppet Master and had made my character stop smoking, she might have evaporated or stopped telling me things, or just been boring. More than likely, she would have just kept smoking and arguing with me about it, which would have been a waste of our time. I know that sounds crazy, but I assure you it is not. I was grateful that she came to me at all.

Non-fiction writers take note as well, because you are often writing your own stories, so it is you who is the main character. Or perhaps it is your beloved heroes you are discussing; maybe they are living heroes, or maybe they are dead. With those you admire most as your main characters, there is a high tendency to project only their best side, and this is even more true if your non-fiction is about you. But, if you can say how you fumbled and fell on your face on occasion, was mean or cruel, did something not so smart, and learned the hard way, or how you were terrified to take the next step, your stories become more compelling and we are more inclined to both believe you, and want to continue reading you. Likewise with your heroes, stories are more compelling if you show not only how they struggled but how their own flaws held them back at times. If you are selling only successes, with no struggle you tend to sound like a bragging blow hard, or a raving fan. In fiction, if the character that you are portraying is too perfect, he or she tends to look like a comic book character or a spoof. In non-fiction, if whoever you are portraying is too good to be real, they are also too good to be relatable.

Even as I write this, I wonder, rightfully, if I am coming off too much like the know it all. But I expect that when I told you the story about my frustrations with my own chain smoking character, and my own spaghetti-ing trials where I hung the themes on the ceiling, and the story of the scene of the two guys in the café that the other writers recognized, this probably helped you understand better that myself and other writers do these crazy things that aren't so crazy. I am willing to bet this made things a little more interesting to read. But if I had just told you that all writers should talk to their characters and asked you to trust me, I doubt it would make you feel you could. The truth is, I don't know if all writers use these techniques or agree with everything I say, but I know most have the same struggles and have discovered these same truths. As I said before, your job is to go through this book and pick out the things that will help you, so I encourage you to try things.

This chapter is about ridding yourself of what you thought writing was. It is to give you permission to get a little crazy and don't always do what you think writing is about. You may have to step outside your comfort zone, so I wanted to give you a few techniques, a few concepts, and some allies to help you. And, it is not me who will be your ally when you get stuck because I won't be there. But your characters will be. And, the Evil Puppet Master who wants to create ego ideals will be there too. I am suggesting "who" you should ask guidance from, and what to try when your writing is just not coming out with the vigor that you had hoped for. Or maybe it's not coming out at all. Go to the vulnerable character(s) within you.

Laying in Bed Writing

If you have been paying attention to every line I have written so far, you would have noticed a couple of references to me lying on my bed and staring up at the ceiling, and I called this writing. Another secret to writing is you do an awful lot of it without actually writing it down. The other news that is not a secret is that eventually you do have to write it down or it doesn't count. But, you could still be writing quite a lot in your head first. I thought this was only true for fiction at first, but it can be equally true for non-fiction. Not everyone will have this ability, or find it works for them, but if you have the ability to tune the surrounding world out and compose things in your head, or just play with ideas and words in your head, or watch the characters in your imagination in your head, then you should give yourself permission to do some lying in bed writing. It's valid and necessary. Some of us need to walk to do this, or I know someone else who needs to drive. The Muse has its favourite places to arrive. The trickier part is knowing when you should switch to writing it down before your mind lets it go in favour of other things.

Capturing your lying in bed writing (or wherever you are doing it), is essential, and you must not presume it will always come back to you when you want. Many a stroke of genius has been lost forever when it was not captured and wrestled to the page. This means you have to recognize when you are doing *in your head writing*, and when you are going to transition it into written words. Usually, this has to be done immediately following your *in your head writing*, at least making good notes, an audio record, a scrawl on the infamous napkin, or something that can bring it back faithfully at a time when you can really work on it. Just make sure it gets captured somehow.

That said, some of us have a continuous saga or some other concepts that keep slowly building in our head for days, weeks and even years, without writing a word. But that is a function of what I call gestation which is slightly different and a place for a new insight into what writing really is, or what it really isn't.

Gestation, Ideas and Planned Revelations

ges·ta·tion (jĕ-stā′shən)
n.
1. The period of development from conception until birth; pregnancy.
2. The conception and development of a plan or an idea in the mind.

In the first writing group I was ever a part of, 20+ years ago, I met a writer, John R. Little, who has since won many prestigious writing awards in the horror genre and published many books. At that time, he was writing many short stories, most of them science fiction, and I was always amazed at how many stories he would come up with. Finally, I asked him how long he usually thought about a story before he wrote it down. Considering he had so many, and seemed so prolific to me, I was expecting that he would say maybe as long as two weeks. I was a little surprised when he said he usually thought about stories for about two years before writing them down. John was the writer who first let me in on the secret called gestation.

Remember how I said that we have many ideas kicking around in our head and some are meant to live and some die and it is similar to how nature builds in the extra numbers to account for the survival rate (or lack of survival rate)? Ideas, characters and storylines are our babies and we create them in extra numbers. But, how many can you hold in your head at once? The answer can be -- and John R. Little is a testament to this -- a whole helluvalot. He was churning out stories every few weeks that he had been gestating for years. That means there were many ideas in there gestating simultaneously.

As I said before, our mind is kind of amazing and will always produce more ideas as long as you are exercising it properly and allow for some creative stretching in your life. So the next question is, how long does it stay in your head gestating before its ready to come out? In nature, there is a range of time that is normal for each species, but for writer's ideas and stories they each have their own timeline for birth. The truth is that many die in the womb. My story about John R. Little is an example of how the gestation period, before you even write a word, can easily be years. I am writing a story now that I anticipate will be more than one book, and have been gestating it for over ten years.

So now you are probably very confused. *Should I keep writing and see if the Muse shows up? Or do I stop writing and keep gestating?* Here is the deal. Always keep writing something. The stories or ideas you have that are not ready will tell you when it is time. You must have faith in the nature of this mysterious process. But remember, unlike nature, it is possible to put something on the page before you are ready, leave it and then go back and revive it another time. That is probably the worst that can happen to you. As long as you don't force it so much you invoke The Evil Puppet Master, or beat yourself up for not finishing, you can try writing something down. But others would say, "wait, wait until you let it reach its full gestation," and they may have a point, this is a creative process after all. But, how do you know that gestation is not our sneaky cold feet procrastination in another form? I am going to try to attempt a guideline for you.

I attempt this guideline under the proviso that it is my own and may not work for all.

I know I am gestating and not procrastinating...

- When I have no fear that I will lose the concept or story without writing it down
- When I know it is a story or concept that takes more thought and I enjoy unrolling it slowly in my mind as a pastime, but not enough pieces are together yet
- When I feel no anxiety at the idea of writing down a few notes in my journal about it (if I felt anxiety at notes, then it may be procrastination).
- When I can't fully see the characters yet or hear their voices (fiction)
- When I am excited about the idea but not enough to write it down yet. There needs to be that nagging desire to write, a feeling of, it's time otherwise keep gestating
- When I am not yet talking to others about it, or doing serious research about it I am still gestating
- When I have no driving purpose or audience to write it down for. If you have a deadline or a driving purpose to get it done faster your motivation feels entirely different. You may have to push through resistance and cut your gestation time down.

On the matter of deadlines, if you are under a deadline and you have to cut your gestation time down drastically, then here is a little trick I discovered when I was taking visual arts classes.

I loved working on larger projects in the studio, but just like in writing sometimes I would get stuck and I didn't want to wreck what I had done so far. I would work in the studio whenever I could during the week with the knowledge that I would have to produce something by end of class on Monday when we had our instructor coming around. I found that if I was frustrated and stuck by Friday, I would decide not to struggle with it any longer and just gestate on it over the weekend, but I would also tell myself *I will have a revelation on Monday morning*. And sure enough positive thinking succeeded. On Monday mornings I would walk into the studio, look at my piece, and have a revelation. I knew exactly what to do next, and by the end of the class I would turn in a completed piece that I liked. I began to call these "Planned Revelations" and yes it works in writing too. So, if you are stuck and perhaps under a timeline, take a short rest, and Plan for a Revelation. What do you have to lose?

Since we are into the realm of ideas and gestation, I want to return to the scary but important reminder that in the end nothing counts unless you write it down. Now if you tell people you are a writer you will start to notice that people come up to you and say the following:

"You are a writer! Say, I have a great idea for a screenplay/novel/book!"
And then they proceed to tell you about it.

When someone does this to me and they finish telling me their idea, I ask the obvious question
"So, are you planning to write this?"

It is at this point that they throw up all their excuses of why they can't and the topic rapidly moves on. If I had $5 for every time I heard this I would be a rich woman. I think this is why accomplished American playwright, Maria Irene Fornes, said, "Ideas are of no use to a writer." It may sound like an extreme thing to say but ideas don't count if you do not act on them. Ideas only survive if you do something with them, and for writers that means words on the page. That is the point where you see how it will come together and how you will really perform the craft of writing. The art of telling an engaging story or communicating a message is ultimately in the writing and the telling, not in the idea or the thinking. So take the chance and put it on the page.

Action vs. Description

We are talking about secrets about writing, and, about writing "not being what you thought it was," and this would not be complete without exploring what kind of writer you are. In working with writers, I find it very useful to divide them in two very broad groups across a spectrum. I can find out quickly which group each writer polarizes toward using two valuable writing exercises. Before doing the exercises, some writers were sure they knew which group they belonged to, and others were not. After the exercises, some were wrong about what they had been sure about, and even if they were not wrong, the exercises gave them a depth of clarity they never had before.

One group is writers who are good at, as well as comfortable writing "descriptions" or "details." The other group is writers who are good at, as well as comfortable writing "action." Although these two groups are not opposites, it is somewhat rare to find writers who are completely comfortable in both camps.

Both of these revealing writing exercises start in the same way. I ask the writers to try to imagine there is a character -- a real person or imagined -- in a room, and they are to write an imaginary scene with this character, but they must stay in the descriptions, and try not to let any action happen. In other words, they are not to move the story forward. They are to describe the details of the character and the room, without the character doing much of anything.

That was exercise one. The next exercise starts the same but is opposite. The writers are now asked to write a scene where the same character, in the same room is constantly in action, doing something, or moving forward (like a Dan Brown novel on steroids), and no effort is spent on description or explanation. These two exercises are done in a short amount of time, maybe ten minutes, and we have a great deal of fun sharing them later. By the end of this, the writers are not only really sure of which camp they belong in, but they are far more clear of how much discomfort one form of writing has for them versus the other. Please feel free to try these exercises yourself, and meanwhile I will explain their value to you and why you want to know how much you polarize to one over the other.

This book is about *Writing with Cold Feet*, or what stops us from writing when it shouldn't. To discover anything that gives us discomfort is valuable. It can help you explain to yourself why you are stuck. In this case, your writing project is demanding you go into either action or description but because it is not your strength you have resistance. If you were uncomfortable in writing descriptions for example, it makes you aware so you can learn how to get comfortable enough with description and details to improve your writing. The other value to this exercise is that whichever effort you are comfortable with, action or description, you can now embrace this as the strength in your writing. It helps you embrace who you are as a writer.

In the book, *Now, Discover Your Strengths* by Marcus Buckingham, Buckingham gives the example of how Tiger Woods dominated the sport of golfing for so long by embracing his strength in driving. He worked on his "short game," pitching and putting, enough to get it to a very good pro level, but went back and focused with his coach on his drive until he became a master at it, able to drive superior distances with great aim and consistency. I am suggesting it is the same with writers. It does not serve us to hate what we don't like, whether it is constructing stories or creating detailed descriptions, but it does serve us to get comfortable enough with them that it helps the rest of our game. We can then really have fun writing what we are good at, our strength, and get better and better at it.

Those who enjoy writing description or details, may enjoy writing poetry, or writing detailed technical manuals, and have a lot of discomfort around writing stories that involve action. However, learning to balance both can only enhance their writing. Even should they choose to write only poetry that shows off their strength, powerful poems often hide stories in them and this is often called prose poetry. In fact, all those Greek Muses that helped all those different kinds of poets (epic poetry, love poetry, sacred poetry…etc.) were really poetic storytellers, the two genres were never divided.

Action writers may be good story creators, adding forward moving action, but they also may skip details that will make them good storytellers. Adding poetic or evocative descriptions may make readers relate to the character better, or extra details may orient their story properly in time and location, and both together give a mood and feeling to the story that elevates it.

Even in non-fiction, a description person who is very good at putting down the details of each step, not forgetting any possible permutations – like a technical manual writer – is not always as good at showing how all these details create an overall concept that is going to make a difference to real people's lives. For that they need to bring out the demonstrator, the actionator, the storyteller. And, by contrast, the action writer in non-fiction may tend to skip over important descriptions that convey the full steps of "how to" or the crux of meaning and importance behind each action.

As you understand what you are most comfortable writing, action or description, you can see the other camp as an ally rather that a reason to stop writing. You have another way to learn how to accomplish your *Writing with Cold Feet.*

Go ahead and start with what you love the most (action or detail) if it gets you writing, but in the next stage you may want to tackle that which isn't as easy, in order for you to get the results you really want. If Tiger Woods let his putting slide, no matter how strong his drive, his game would be way down. So, you may want to learn to embrace both and use the action or description exercises to help you. For example, if you have written a beautiful passage for your book but realize it is not getting to the action soon enough, use the exercise to write all action, as uncomfortable as it may feel, just to move your story forward. Likewise, when I am charging forward in a story (because I am an action gal), I have to stop and go back and practice painstaking detail for awhile. I may not use all of it, but I will always use some of it, and be grateful that I do shift myself to that place because my writing does get better.

The most spectacular revelation I ever saw from anyone who did these exercises was a writer who had already finished a novel, but was completely unsatisfied with it. When she tried the action and description exercises, she found out that she was a description person who had difficulty staying in action. She understood why she was so unsatisfied with her novel. It was, by her own admission, 140 pages of mostly description with a story that wasn't going anywhere. It had not been fully developed as a true story. If she had at least gone into action more, and also understood the elements of story, it would have been easier to develop a story from her characters.

To be honest, with the possible exception of some technical writing, I think the action people have an advantage over the detail people. It is easy to get lost in description and not move a story or concept forward when it should. But, you can always add description later. It is hard to add story or concepts later. Even poets need to add a purpose, through-line or progression to their poetic thoughts. The point here is to make you aware of your strengths and your discomforts, and try to balance them and bring them up to a practical level (Tiger Woods' short game). When you make both sides reasonably comfortable for yourself, then you stop blocking and see an improvement in your writing. Should you choose not to do this, then there are other solutions which involve adding others to your process.

If you are having trouble with your story because you are a description person, start reading books from story experts, or story structure experts. My own system is called *The Power of Story* and has versions for both fiction and non-fiction writers. If the books aren't helping you, then you may want to work with an editor, mentor, writing teacher, story coach, consultant or story doctor, to get you on the right track story wise, and then you can have more fun with the description. But, if you are a story person who beats themselves up for not putting enough care into grammar and description, remember you can get professional help with that later. For now, go with your strength and write that story with wonderful abandon.

I know of two writers with different strengths who like to collaborate with one another. These two make it work by one writing mostly the plot and the other writing mostly the descriptions. If this seems an unusual collaboration maybe you should consider that all serious writers have collaborators. All of us have to collaborate with editors. We love to use editors and if we don't, we soon will, so let's have a word about editors.

Editors

Many people confuse editors with proofreaders. I am embarrassed to say that I once chastised my editor for missing some minor errors in spacing. However, I was later educated that editors and proofreaders are not the same thing and nor should they be. Editors may proofread enroute, but that is not actually why they are there. Editors usually edit for better flow and that often means "less is more." They are often suggesting quicker and smoother ways to say something, as well as questioning any confusing or contradicting statements they may see. It is only after an editor has edited, that you will want to get a number of people to proofread your work, whether they are professionals or amateurs. That's what your anal, detail-obsessed friends are great for. But they are not editors.

A true editor brings out the best in your work, and different editors have different strengths. Some may be very good at reading a whole book and seeing where major changes to the body will help. They may switch the order of topics, or may want to make major cuts, or ask you for additions that will improve the product. They may just ask you profound questions that subtlety point out that you haven't thought something through about your piece. These editing suggestions may be done by agents or publishers as well. Other editors will just look at the flow of your existing text and improve it. Some are great at fact checking. Some are stupendously good at grammar. The point is, there will always be people around who are better at all these details than you could be, plus they will be able to approach your work with an objective eye. What does this mean? Don't let the details or the editing chore interrupt you too much in the midst of your writing progress.

If you are an editor type, but today you are a writer, you may want to ask your left internal editor to take a break at times and let your right brain go crazy and churn out more words. Always promise your left brain editor that they can have their time later. We may have trouble finishing if we allow too much stopping and correcting, but even detail writers need editors. Their editors will often cut through too much perfection details and over-explanation to get to the simple truths the writer is trying to get to. It's like clearing out the clutter so you can see the beauty of the room.

Those of you who are not at all detail people will really love editors too, as they spin your raw material into a smooth flow without the rough edges. If nothing else, editors are a wonderful relief that writing doesn't have to be done all alone. So, if you hire an editor, or meet one, hug them.

This chapter has been about realizing that writing is not always what you thought it was (and you don't do all of it alone). Now you can start embracing the idea in our next chapter, *The Secrets of Letting Go.*

4

the secrets of letting go

Letting Go

I remember the first, last, and only time I ever tried to water ski. Everyone was cheerful and smiling in the paradise that was summer at Lake Okanagan. I watched one person launch on the water skis, and after a successful run, glide into the shore. It convinced me to try, because it looked easy, graceful and great fun. "Remember to lean back," they all told me as they strapped me in the skis and gave me the rope tow handle. What happened next others blamed on the boat driver starting off too slow, but all I remember was water slugging me in the face in a very unpleasant way as I was dragged forward. Slowly my brain heard the cries around me, "Let go! Let go!" And, finally I let go.
Later they asked, "Why didn't you let go sooner?"
I said, "Because no one told me I might have to let go at the beginning."

This third section of *Writing with Cold Feet* is about the secrets of letting go. I am going to assume that no one told you that writing was about letting go. There are a number of things we have already discussed that are features of letting go, like letting go of perfectionism or letting go of The Evil Puppet Master, but there are a few more secrets about letting go and freeing the writer within that you may want to know.

Lying

From a young age we are schooled not to lie, but the human condition, being what it is, sometimes we do lie a little. We lie about our weight, our age, our income, whether we are busy on Friday night, whether we are "still mad" at someone, or the fact that we don't really know the difference between a Merlot and a Shiraz. Whether we lie for justifiable reasons or ego, we may feel a small pang of guilt or discomfort knowing that it's a fib. We want to be honest, try to be truthful and strive to be accurate. But, how would you like to be able to abandon that burden and have guilt-free lying? And not just little lies, big ones. Add a few zeros to the old income, make up some big nasty lies about that person at work who ticks you off, let people know that you are getting calls from celebrities clamouring for your attention, tell people you've been to a country when you don't even know what continent it's on, and speak languages fluently that you can barely say hello in. Do all this, and not get caught. You can. In writing, this is not lying, it's fiction.

Given this freedom, it is amazing how many writers let their imaginations stay in a box and keep things pretty average or closed. And I'm talking about the fiction writers. Even in non-fiction, embellishment is necessary to add colour, depth and interest to a non-fiction story. To get out of this box, what you are going to want to let go of is the idea of accuracy. No one loves a great storyteller for their accuracy. Or, another way to put it is, don't let too many facts get in the way of a good story. Whether it is un-provable details in a based-on-truth story, or pure fiction, remember to tell a good yarn the way you want to tell it, or the way it might best be told to generate excitement. Who gets excited about accuracy really? Accountants and bowlers? And even they long for a good story.

It may help you to remember that truth is often stranger than fiction. Film director, Paul Morrisey, told me that when writing his film, *Beethoven's Nephew,* he had to change the truth because it was too unbelievable. Historians documented that in a suicide attempt made by the nephew of Ludwig van Beethoven, he not only put one pistol to his head, but two pistols in each hand, and missed with both. Morrisey said it looked and seemed too ridiculous to be true. So he cut it back to one gun because it wasn't adding to the story he was telling.

Every story can use a little embellishment and the storyteller's license in either direction. Unless you are under scrupulous ethical, academic or professional codes, let the accuracy go and no longer think of every story as truth with a small "t," but look for the Truth with the large "T" that your audience needs and will learn better when the story is well told. If you and no one else can possibly know the gaps in the "true" story – make it up. Use your imagination.

Even in historical documentations, it has been proven time and again that we cannot always depend on the writers of them for accuracy. They have been, and will continue to be, bent for political, religious, or other reasons, including old fashioned prejudice. Therefore you can use your conscience with your imagination to portray what is really True, or what should be True. In the process, if you can greatly entertain us, and use some common sense and don't deliberately try to commit libel or fraud for personal gain, all is forgiven. In the famous satirical essay, *A Modest Proposal,* by Jonathan Swift, Swift ridiculously suggested a plan for eating poor Irish children. He did this to make a much needed political and human rights point, which would not have had the intended impact or be lauded as a great piece of writing if the writer hung on to our "never lie" bonds. Likewise, Nellie McClung, author and famous Canadian suffragette, used a similar technique in her infamous speech of the day entitled Why *Men Should Not Be Allowed to Vote.*

In short, you are a writer, your power is stronger and more enduring than swords and you have permission to do whatever you want. Let go and lie away.

Mom Won't Like It

I read a story in which a man at age 40 was still wearing the clothes his mother bought for him because he didn't want to offend her. If you are still under the tyranny of worrying about what your family thinks, when you really have some different ideas entirely, maybe you will want to find a therapist to work on that. But to be honest, we all have people who are close to us who think they know us because they have been around since our beginning. But they don't really know us. Many budding writers are stifled by the idea of letting friends and family in on an entirely different side of themselves. For other artists this may be less of a problem perhaps, but the literal nature of writing may make this scarier. This is especially true if you are writing about real events that happened to you and involve real people who are still living.

I have known people who are waiting until someone is dead before they are going to write. People are often worried about telling a story, a true story, just in case a person, or persons involved reads it and flips out. Now this may seem like a legal point, and in some cases it is, but often it is extraneous worry that we need to let go of. I have written about true events with potentially touchy subjects and worried, knowing full well that the people depicted in it were going to read it. I worried a great deal. I may have even tried to soften it, went back and forth, and finally put back the bits that made it a good story, as bold as they may have been. I struggled. But I let go. And, to my surprise, frequently the person did not recognize themselves, or couldn't remember the episode, or thought it was just great. It was worth it to let go and see the results, because it gives you permission to keep telling your story.

There are all kinds of sneaky ways to get around depicting a real person or organization before you even think about any need to involve legal advice. First, change the names. This may seem obvious but I have had to advise this before. Unless you are writing a full exposé on a public figure, professional person, company or an individual, in which case you will want lawyers, then why do you have to retain the person or company's real name? Your Truth with a capital "T" should not be dependent on real names.

After changing the names, here are three more tips for writing about others without getting in trouble. Tip number two is, change the sex of the person if it makes no difference to the story. Surprisingly, it often works very well. Third tip, in your own stories, change their relationship to you. In other words, make it an acquaintance who said or did "XYZ" and not your sister! Fourth tip, although I've never used it, there is the "small penis rule" allegedly used by novelist Michael Crichton to get back at a nasty reviewer. The strategy is that the man who you are taking from reality and revealing something unflattering even libelous about them, in Creighton's case the reviewer, you also happen to mention that they have a really small penis. Either that, or something else significantly embarrassing that they won't really want to defend it in a court of law, where they would have to admit that this character was a very recognizable albeit libellous version of themselves. Isn't fiction wonderful!

The gist of this is, if you are waiting until someone dies or it seems safe to write what you need to write, recognize this as an excuse to not write. There are always ways around these things, so let go of your fears and worries and write it.

Let it Be Bad

How I love to do the "let it be bad" exercise in a classroom. This is where I get writers to try and write something awful. Very much like the "Wrecking It" lesson under *Resistance and Other Pitfalls*, if you try to write something bad it often comes out good, or at the very worst makes you realize that you know the difference between bad and good and you should stop worrying and start letting go of whether you might be bad or good all the time because you are never going to be that bad. Okay.

When I give this exercise, and let people try to be bad for a 20 minute writing period, we just about die laughing reading the results later. Sure they are funny, campy, and often melodramatic, but they are also outrageously good, proving that if you go way over the top it can really pay off. It gives people permission to break rules that they didn't even know they were held back by. As examples, one of my students chose to write his prose in spectacular and shocking headlines. It started out as hilarious tabloid talk but came out in the end as a rather poignant comment on our society. Another student did a depiction of a desperate-for-a-man woman in the throws of unrequited love. The scene had a failed suicide threat in it, but also a reversal at the end where she moves on from the man she has been pursuing, just as he suddenly has a change of heart and wants her. It was an ironic and funny comment on love and the chase.

Only one thing left to say: let go of being good. Bad is good. Liberate yourself. Discover what's there when you take those shackles off.

No One Knows If You Made a Mistake

As a presentation coach, when working with public speakers, I usually have to pry their speech notes away from them. Often, they say, "But I am afraid I will forget something and make a mistake!"
"Does the audience have your notes?" I ask.
"No."
"Then how will they know you've forgotten something or made a mistake?" This stops them.

Believe in your own words and message rather than the order the words are put on the page. This is a great liberation. Writers need this liberation. No one can say you've made a mistake. We have already discussed that you can get an editor and proof-reader's help for any of those technical or grammar mistakes, so other than that, you can't make a mistake. And, this is the truly beautiful part, even if you think it is a mistake, no one will know you made a mistake unless you say so. Even for grammar, who says it is correct? I tell all my editors that I consciously use sentence fragments, so please don't correct them. That's right. Fragments rule. They are my style rather than cramping it. Can you make a mistake about expressing your opinion? If so, this book is riddled with my mistakes, but who would know?

Like letting go of being good, you can let go of the idea of making mistakes or omissions. If you become obsessed with them, the book, the story, the work may never be accomplished, and that is the saddest mistake of all.

Do I have Anything New to Add?

Literature is not exhaustible, for the sufficient and simple reason that a single book is not. A book is not an isolated entity: it is a narration, an axis of innumerable narrations. One literature differs from another, either before or after it, not so much because of the text as for the manner in which it is read."
- Jorge Luis Borges, writer, essayist & poet

Just typing the heading of this section scares me to pieces and brings up old demons. *What if I don't have anything new to add to the world? What if it's all been said and done before? What if someone beat me to this important message I have?"* We all may feel like this at times. And sometimes people will out and out say to us in a very glib and judgmental tone, "What's different about your message?" Again, stop worrying. First, it is true that all the universal Truths have been said and done before. And, it is also true that they always need to be said again. How you say them is important to you, important to your readers, and important to your generation. Sure, you should research the competition, strive to find something you believe and something that is yours. Everyone does this as a mark of being an individual and an artist, but don't let it hold you back if others have similar messages.

Your message may be similar and may be different too, but your stories should always be unique. My story of being invited to the poet, Ulrich Schaffer's home, without knowing who he was, was unique to me. Remember when I said all writers are entrepreneurs? It is good marketing to play up your uniqueness, but sometimes a non-fiction book is memorable for only one or two unique stories or examples that lie within it. They are the goodies that the author has either discovered, or they are her own stories. We call these signature stories that are unique to the author and make a book, speech or article shine.

If you write fiction, no two stories are ever the same, so it comes back to the issue of having confidence in your words, your characters, and your world. Only you have the key to that world, no one else. Sure you want to make sure the story has drama and the characters have depth, but that is why we study our craft. The essence of the story will be unique to you. So let go of the idea that you may not have anything new to add. By virtue of being you, it is unique.

Telling Stories - Sharing

When I first start a class off, often I will get the writers to tell stories before they write them. Why? Because we are social creatures and love to share and get instant feedback in the form of laughter, Ahas, sighs, smiles, questions and anything else we can get. But if you are too precious about your words, afraid someone will steal them, or judge them, or say something unkind, you may not know it, but you are suffering a great loss. The greatest joys come from the joy of sharing. It is a risk, but it is a risk that ultimately has no downsides. The worst is you learn something about yourself, about your style, about your story, about how you communicate, about who you are, or about who your readers or listeners are. Sharing is good.

My partner loves to tell the story of a famous author, before she was famous, who thought the story she had been working on for ten years was crap. Much in the story had parallels to her own life but it was a story set in the generation before her, her mother and grandmother's. One of the women in her circle said she was too silly to write a book and she was often teased about how she was never going to show her boring tome to anyone, so on an impulse she gave it to an editor she knew. She told him that it was incomplete but she was letting him see it, so he'd better take it before she changed her mind. And the next day she did change her mind and demanded it back. But the editor would not give it back. He had read enough to know that what she had was unique and with great potential. They worked together on it but eventually she received an advance and it was published. For awhile it outsold the only other greatest bestseller: the bible. It was made into a movie that gave her the highest amount for movie rights at the time, $50,000 in 1938. The movie received ten academy awards and ensured the book to be a classic and continued bestseller. The author was Margaret Mitchell and the book was *Gone with the Wind.* Although she had been a columnist for a small publication, it was the only book Mitchell was to ever publish in her lifetime and it almost didn't see the light of day. She had the key to the life and world of one of the most famous literary characters in history, Scarlett O'Hara, and she told herself for years that it wasn't a special enough story for anyone else to be interested. So, the question becomes are you *Writing with Cold Feet* because you think your story may not be special enough? Remember only you have the key to your mind, your imagination, your experiences, your stories, your thoughts and your Muse. And the only way you can share them, whether they are unique or not, is by getting them out there, and that is the ultimate letting go.

Support, Writer's Groups and Oversupport

Where do you let go and share? How about friends, family, clubs, contests, newsletters, blogs, writing classes, writing groups and damn near anyone who will listen? Sometimes I think the journey of writers is to leap frog all the way along into larger and larger groups to share with. Some people stay quite content with a smallish group for a long time before they shift. Sometimes it is because something they write has the right timing for it to "break through" into a larger audience, but it can also mean that something in them has changed and they are ready to let go of one level and move to another. It may mean they have learned that all authors are entrepreneurs and they have started marketing their own wares. But on that leap-frogging journey no one ever gets sick of hearing that their words meant something to someone. So, never stop telling others too. Sharing and support is invaluable. And there is one more lesson about support and letting go that may seem harsh, but it is that sometimes you have to let go of the support itself to leapfrog to the next level. If you are too dependent, I call this oversupport.

I have seen people enter writers' groups or go to writers' conferences annually and love all the ideas, and networking and knowledge they get and then never push away from them. At some point you need to say no to testing the waters, going to workshops, getting more feedback, and just get down to the business of writing. You can always go back, but maybe you should move on before you make that call.

When I hold my writers' retreat I always give time, even in our class time, for the writers to write. Writers are expected to leave the group and do more writing on their own. But inevitably, at the beginning, resistance arises for many of them, as if they expected that I was somehow going to write their words for them. Retreats are *time* to write and if you are not writing you are not using it for the essential thing.

And, guess what, after a retreat, after you have given yourself a chunk of time to write or what Brendon Burchard calls chunking, you still have to find more time to write, polish, edit, market and work with people you trust. This is a kind of new support, but this support is less dependent and more self-directed. You will now employ people versus hanging around them.

Oversupport is kind of like seeing someone recovering from an injury who has relied too much on crutches, orthopaedics, or other manufactured body support systems and therefore the muscles have never had a chance to get strong. You, as a writer, need to start to polish your process without perpetually gathering more information and returning to things that may have become too familiar. Honour your support, but stick to the essential things that work for you, and be prepared to let go of some habits that you have outgrown. It's a good thing to know you are now too strong to need these.

4

the last secret – your process

Process

There is a famous story about the legendary actor, Sir Lawrence Olivier. One night he was playing Hamlet and the performance was sublime and it transported the audience. With the "Bravos!" still ringing in the theatre and many curtain calls having been demanded, the actor went into his dressing room where his dresser awaited him. As soon as he stepped into the dressing room he started ripping things apart, swearing and smashing things in his dressing room. The dresser, seeing his master in such anguish said, "Sir, I don't understand, you were brilliant tonight." To which Olivier replied, "Yes, but I don't know why."

Olivier was furious because he knew that for actors and all artists to know when, how and why they are going to do their best work is gold. People seek a formula for "success" but perhaps what we should seek is our formula, or our process. This book has shown many elements of process, some that work for many, some that work for a few, but there are some things that work for only one. Like both *Zorro*'s or the *Lone Ranger*'s horses, Tornado and Silver, who would not let another man sit on their backs, some things will only be for you. These faithful horses are known as Your Process, and whether your style is dark (Tornado), or light (Silver), how you ride that animal will be yours alone.

One does not learn one's process by sitting on the sidelines and thinking about it, one has to mount the horse and keep getting back on it when you fall off. And we all fall off. The sooner a writer starts to discover her or his process – what works, what doesn't – the sooner writing and the greater enjoyment of it flows.

I am constantly correcting people that say they want to learn how to write. They do not need to learn how to write. They have known since grade school how to write. They need to learn how they want to write, and how they best write for themselves. Writing has surprisingly little to do with grammar or sentence structure contrary to what many of us initially thought. Sure you need to know basics, but there are many who get tripped up in the details and the perfectionism, so forge ahead. Learn by doing.

I had a writer (who wasn't sure he was a writer) show up to my writing retreat and tell me that he had just bought a CD entitled *How to Write a Perfect Sentence*, but he didn't have a chance to get to it before he arrived (thankfully). Right then, I knew then the saboteur called perfectionism was going to be an issue with him. The man had an incredible wealth of knowledge and stories in his head that he had been churning over for many years (gestation). It was easy to get him to talk about them, but each time I tried to encourage him to "write it down," and start generating pages, the old resistances and perfectionism came up. Even as consciously he started to recognize it, the knowledge yielded minimal results when left on his own to write.

One day, I made a conscious choice to get tough, and lay it on the line to him privately. He and I had "words" one morning that were not of the literary kind. This was something one of my mentors had done for me once. My mentor imposed a deadline on me and said that if I failed to meet it he said he would have to "help me write it." This had so cut to my pride that I kicked it up a notch and produced some of my best and most voluminous work. I know that this pushing and threatening style will not work for everyone, but I felt this particular writer could take it. So I held my breath as I laid it on the line to him to have something ready for a reading that night if he wanted to be a part of this retreat. That night, as the retreat writers gathered for a happy evening meal in which the reading was to follow, he was nowhere to be seen. In my nervousness of whether I had done the right thing, I confessed to a couple of writers that I may have pushed him too far.

But he arrived in a few minutes later and when it came time to read he said he wanted to preface his reading by saying something. He told the others that he had been a football coach for many years and he knew that a good coach had to sometimes push his players to get the best out of them. He then said that I had done that for him today and he had written several pages. He then brought out a delightful ceramic frog, painted in brilliant colors and gave it to me as a gift, this frog did not say, "ribit, ribit," this frog said, "write it, write it," and became the official mascot to the retreat. He then proceeded to read what he had written which was one of his most fascinating and heart-felt stories of a cold case that had haunted him from his days as a police officer. I had been encouraging him to write it ever since he had told it to me. It was a gripping story in which people listened to every word. It generated a great deal of sincere praise. This was the most personal, moving story they had heard from him so far. They wanted to know more. He learned that he did have an important message in his stories that people really responded to.

After this episode he found that he started to write much more easily without being pushed or prodded by anyone, least of all me. "It's just flowing," he told me, "and I am surprised how much I know and how much I have to say." I was not surprised because he had been saying it all along, just not writing it. He started to generate pages, consciously putting his perfectionist aside. What he discovered about his process was 1) that the perfectionist in him gave him a large block of resistance, and that he would need to break through it each time it arose, 2) he needed to tell his most meaty stories first to get the juices flowing – he had been trapped by chronology and how to organize material up until that point, 3) he needed to have an immediate audience to convince him that he did have an important message and his writing had impact. And 4) he also told me he discovered that he was a visual organizer and felt trapped by the computer screen, but when he realized that he could have things on several pages, out in front of him, this helped. Also that he could leave some of the organization to the middle and end parts of his process, and not insist on it all being mapped out at the beginning. When he stuck to the writing he could believe he was going to be able to complete his book.

The following are questions to help you reveal who you are as a writer, and what your own secret process may be. With this knowledge you may begin to be actively involved in creating and discovering your process. When you finish answering the questions, my advice is to toss them into the back of your head for now, and then periodically review them. You will discover the true answers over time. You will change your answers or add to them. But for now, you just need to bring them from the unconscious mind into the conscious mind. REMEMBER: there are no wrong answers because it is *your* process.

Questions to Help You Discover Your Process

1. Are you more comfortable writing Action? Or are you more comfortable writing Descriptive Detail?
2. How does the previous knowledge effect your process?
3. When and how do you show up for your writing? (80% of success is...)
4. What are your methods for working through your resistance?
5. Are you conscious of when you procrastinate and how to gently work through it?
6. What are your biggest lies you tell yourself for why you cannot write? (e.g.: time, money, laziness...)
7. How are you going to put those lies to rest each time they arise?
8. Are you a chunker, or do you find time daily to write, or a bit of both? How do you distribute your time so it works for you?
9. What are the things that most make you want to write? (e.g..: playing with words, sharing with an audience, getting lost in another world, etc.)
10. Have you figured out how to regularly include the things that make you most want to write in your life to help you stay motivated?
11. How do you organize and when?
12. What are your habits before you meet deadlines?
13. When and how do you rest between writing? What rituals or routines do you indulge in that enhance your writing experience (and results)?
14. What is your process for research? How much do you do when, and when do you reduce it to only fact checking?
15. How do you explore and get to know your characters and their motivations?
16. (For fiction) How strictly or loosely do you consciously use a story structure and when do you start it, leave it, and return to it?
17. (For non-fiction) How strictly or loosely do you consciously use an outline and when do you start it, leave it, and return to it?
18. When do you look for your theme, central message(s), goals, or through-lines, to help you stay on track?
19. How do you know when you are gestating or procrastinating?

You may realize by the previous questions that we have touched on all of these subjects in previous chapters. All of it is relevant to your process and many other things besides. A process is repeatable once you know it. If Sir Lawrence Olivier had known what he had done that night to have a brilliant performance, surely he would have repeated it as much as he could. So, even if the process is how to best seduce your mysterious Muse, the trick will be to find the pick-up lines that always work. Avoid the things that turn your Muse off, and endure the joys and pains of courtship with him or her. Remember to try switching it up to keep you both on your toes, but keep discovering what works. This is your true work and the last secret to *Writing with Cold Feet*.

The Most Blocked Writer Ever

Now, you have all the secrets. Yet, I have one last story about the weirdness and wonderfulness of being a writer. This is about a blocked writer. One that has been called the most blocked writer in history, although I seriously doubt that is true.

Fran Lebowitz is supposedly still working on a book that was commissioned more than 20 years ago, and her publishers are still waiting. Fran has admitted her love of talking, and her dislike of writing. She is a very sharp and witty person who dazzles with her many off-the-cuff remarks. Though known as an author she has written only a scant five books in her whole career (and some of those were compilations), but Lebowitz has garnered fame and has been in the limelight for a very, very long time in the New York City milieu.

Martin Scorsese directed a documentary about Lebowitz called, *Public Speaking* because of Lebowitz's unending speaking appearances. Some have said that she has made a career of writing by not writing. My belief is that Lebowitz does not need to complete that book she has been promising for 20 years as long as she can get her satisfaction in front of an audience. Look back at the #9 question in my list to help you discover your process, *What makes you want to write?* Lebowitz's answers to that question might be, "sharing with an audience" and "gaining recognition" and as long as those are satisfied in other ways, she may never finish that book, nor should she. Yet, her quantity of written or unwritten books may not be the issue, the issue is still one of process.

After admitting she has a fear of writing, Lebowitz has said, "The act of writing puts you in confrontation with yourself, which is why I think writers assiduously avoid writing… It's much more relaxing actually to work." How many of us agree that working, checking things off a task list, is much easier than writing? Writing is scarier and a place of self discovery. But, for many of us, talking in front of others and writing speeches can also be a very scary place, and a place of self discovery. Note that Lebowitz, while struggling with writing, is still writing something to speak about, and still connecting with an audience and thus her readers. Lebowitz also describes writers as warriors, and writing as the reward both during the process and after. She says about writing that the battle is… "The rewards of any warrior. The word that best describes my feeling of having written is *triumphant* — triumphant on the level of Alexander the Great. Having overcome your worst fear, the thing you are most vulnerable to, that is the definition of heroic. Also, it's such a worthwhile human activity. The most."[ii]

I agree with Lebowitz that writing is, at the very least, one of the most "worthwhile human activities," especially in contrast to many other activities, housekeeping, for example. I dislike housekeeping and cleaning, but I love having a clean place. The times when I have employed a maid and have come home to a place that is completely clean and tidy, you have never seen a person so ecstatically happy. You'd think I'd won an award or something. I love the cleanliness, the orderliness, the lack of dust, the clean surfaces, the sense that all is right in my little world. And, most of all, not only do I not give a fig that another woman or man did this for me, au contraire, I am really happy that someone else did the work so I didn't have to. This would not be the same for writing.

If I came home and someone else had done my writing, I would not be happy at all. Quite the opposite. Even, if it was excellent writing that I admired and was allowed to attach my name to it, guilt free, I would not like it. Even if I wrote it myself, but in a bout of amnesia could not remember the act of writing it, it would not be the same.

Much like Stephen King's admission that his alcoholism was a regret because he could not remember the process of writing some of his books, I would miss it. I would miss the aha! moments. I would miss the sense of connection. I would miss the frustration, followed by the breakthrough. I would miss the sense of discovery. I would miss the ability to immerse myself in another world. I would miss the sound of my fingers on the keyboard in a passionate flurry of keystrokes because I can't type as fast as the words are coming. I would miss the anticipation of sharing what I'm writing that often comes even while I am still writing it. There is no way I would give that up for anyone or anything.

There does seem to be this universal fear of writing, or I would not have been given that fateful assignment many years ago to teach that fear of writing class. I, for one, am happy that I have been given the gift of that fear which gives me the greater gift to perpetually overcome it. I hope that I, and all who consider themselves reluctant writers, will never let the fear win and will instead move forward and continue *Writing with Cold Feet.*

Quotes to Remember

From *Writing with Cold Feet* by Kathrin Lake

"Being a writer is like being a gardener. You are a writer because you write, just like a gardener is a gardener because they have been gardening, not for any other reason."

"A writer has to learn how to be their own biggest fan."

"... you have to have a thick skin and a thin skin at the same time. In other words, you have to listen to your feedback with your armor on, and choose what you will take in. "

"Writers need permission to get a little crazy and not do what they expect writing to be."

"All writers are entrepreneurs whether they know it or not."

"Don't let too many facts get in the way of a good story."

"No one loves a great storyteller for their accuracy… Who gets excited about accuracy really? Accountants and bowlers? And even they long for a good story."

"Never underestimate the power of your characters."

"When your writing is just not coming out with the vigour that you had hoped for, go to the vulnerable characters within you."

"…No one ever gets sick of hearing that their words meant something to someone."

"Often, as writers, we cannot see beyond our own intentions or ego ideals. We cannot see when the work itself needs to lead, not us. But if you listen, it can tell you what to feed it."

"One does not learn one's process for writing by sitting on the sidelines and thinking about it, one has to mount the horse and keep getting back on it when you fall off. And we all fall off."

"The times when I have employed a maid and have come home to a place that is completely clean and tidy, you have never seen a person so ecstatically happy. You'd think I'd won an award or something... If I came home and someone else had done my writing, I would not be happy at all."

INDEX

FOOTNOTES

[i] Quote from Dr. Joseph Ferrari in Procrastination and Task Avoidance: theory, research and treatment by Joseph Ferrari, Judith Johnson, Willian McCowan, Plenium Press, Springer, New York, 1995

[ii] All quotes from Fran Lebowitz come from "Fran Lebowitz, A Humorist at Work" Interviewed by James Linville and George Plimpton, for The Paris Review, #127, Summer 1993.

About the Author

When Kathrin was eight, she made up stories, cast the other kids in parts, raided her mother's closet and then started rehearsals immediately. Much later she studied theatre and film at Simon Fraser University in Vancouver, B.C. Although she developed a passion for non-fiction by writing for the campus newspaper and then other publications, it was being in the Theatre that reignited her storytelling days as a child. She collaborated with award-winning Canadian playwrights Marc Diamond and Guillermo Verdecchia, and even formed a brief writing partnership with the late, great comedy writer, Irwin Barker, who would go on to write for Rick Mercer (in Canada that is equivalent to working for David Letterman). She even started winning some awards and prizes herself in playwriting. On a dare, she also started a community newspaper in Vancouver called The Drive in the happening arts neighborhood of the same name.

Kathrin founded *The Vancouver School of Writing* and is a full time writer, story coach and professional speaker. Her first non-fiction book was *From Survival to Thrival*, but in addition to *Writing with Cold Feet* she has also written The *A to Zen of Writing* book series. She frequently holds seminars about writing and publishing such as, *How to Write and Publish Your eBook in 21 days*.

http://www.kathrinlake.com
http://www.vancouverschoolofwriting.com

CPSIA information can be obtained
at www.ICGtesting.com
Printed in the USA
FSOW02n2015010915
10649FS